Our Shining Legacy

To Attendees at

The Association of African American Financial Advisors

2022 Annual National Conference in Atlanta, GA

Read, enjoy and be inspired by this book that recounts a family's entrepreneurial and educational legacy in Richmond, Virginia. Despite the prejudice and bigotry they endured, three generations of Wallers and Dungees persisted. They developed a jewelry trade, built other businesses, secured an education and supported their families.

The International Afro-American Historical and Genealogical Society (AAHGS) selected *Our Shining Legacy* as the 2021 Winner: Non-Fiction: Historical Category in recognition of the highly acclaimed book.

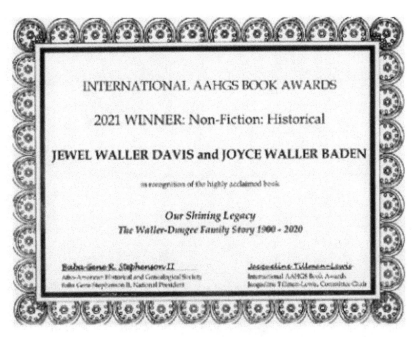

INTERNATIONAL AAHGS BOOK AWARDS

2021 WINNER: Non-Fiction: Historical

JEWEL WALLER DAVIS and JOYCE WALLER BADEN

in recognition of the highly acclaimed book

Our Shining Legacy
The Waller-Dungee Family Story 1900 - 2020

Baba-Gene R. Stephenson II
Afro-American Historical and Genealogical Society
Baba Gene Stephenson II, National President

Jacqueline Tillman-Lewis
International AAHGS Book Awards
Jacqueline Tillman-Lewis, Committee Chair

Jewel Waller Davis and Joyce Waller Baden

Praise for *Our Shining Legacy*

A "MUST READ" FOR ALL AMERICANS!

Written at a time in U.S. history when hatred, bigotry and fear have spiraled downward and created an atmosphere of distrust and hopelessness, *Our Shining Legacy* reads like a much-needed breath of fresh air! For those who have only been able to see African Americans through a media-created lens of suspicion and stereotypes, this book shatters those negative tropes and tells a powerful story of how a Black family, with faith in God, determination and a belief in integrity, was able to overcome tremendous racist odds and not only pass on a love for education, but also transmit values that included an incredible sense of hope and love for all people (regardless of their color, creed or ethnicity) while achieving what the odds would have said were impossible goals.

For 120 years the Black-founded and Black-owned Waller family jewelry business has stood first on Leigh Street and then in the heart of downtown Richmond, Virginia, the home of the Confederacy. It is a testament to what hard work and faith in God can do in spite of hate and Jim Crow laws during the early 1900s. African Americans need this book "for such a time as this." All Americans need this book "for such a time as this." Read it! Enjoy it and be blessed by it!

Dr. Jeremiah Wright Jr., Pastor Emeritus
Trinity United Church of Christ, Chicago, Illinois

OUR SHINING LEGACY UNCOVERS THE TRUTH

It has been said, "A mind is a terrible thing to waste." We were all created by God to think and to learn. The desire to know, the yearning for knowledge, to know the "what" and the "how" are a part of the human DNA. The people of Africa did not stop their desire for knowledge simply because they were brought to the Americas and enslaved. The mind is always searching for knowledge and seeking understanding.

Throughout this sad history of Blacks in America, there were points of light recorded about how slaves were secretly taught to read and write. Therefore, it was no surprise to me when I read about Fannie Aribelle Williams Dungee, a free-woman, being awarded her diploma from the Richmond Colored Normal School in 1900, just 35 years after the end of the Civil War and 23 years after the end of Reconstruction. *Our Shining Legacy* chronicles the history of a family determined to become self-reliant, educated and entrepreneurial. This entrepreneurial legacy can be traced to Marcellus Carrington Waller, who was born in 1873 and, in 1900, established the clock, watch and jewelry repair business. This family legacy chronicles an important part of the great history of the gifts, talents and determination of African American people.

Our Shining Legacy uncovers the truth about people of African heritage and our zeal for knowledge, to prosper and to be self-supporting individuals within the greater community of the human family.

As you read this book, please note that from the seeds planted by Absalom and Eliza Waller and by Mary Robinson and Oliver Williams, in the late 1800s, the transmission of the desire for knowledge has continued, unbroken, through five generations. Indeed, education is an enduring Waller-Dungee family value. This book will bring to light and to life the many families whose stories will never be published, but will shine through this recorded history and legacy. *Our Shining Legacy* will serve as a guidepost for generations who will journey this way.

Hiawatha Boykin Fountain, Ph.D., Associate Superintendent (Retired)
Montgomery County Public Schools, Rockville, Maryland

OUR SHINING LEGACY

THE WALLER-DUNGEE FAMILY STORY 1900 – 2020

Clockwise: M.C. Waller Sr., grandfather; Mary Williams, great-grandmother; Jesse M. Dungee Sr. and Fannie Williams Dungee, grandparents; Lillian Dungee Henderson, aunt; Richard A. Waller Sr. and Florence Dungee Waller, parents

JEWEL WALLER DAVIS & JOYCE WALLER BADEN

ISBN: 978-0-578-84634-7 (Paperback)
ISBN: 978-0-578-88653-4 (Hardcover)

First printing edition 2020

Printed by Ingram Spark
www.IngramSpark.com

Published by Jewel Waller Davis and Joyce Waller Baden,
in the United States of America.

Our Shining Legacy
P.O. Box 142
Riva, MD 21140
United States

OurShiningLegacy@gmail.com

Contents

Epilogue

Foreword

Early Africans in America, like their forebears, were of great intellect as well as expert artisans in mainline crafts practiced by freeborn and freed enslaved souls. The rise of African Americans in business, in the professions and in inventive thought was promising. Showing unexpected progress in the face of overwhelming odds, they utilized their skill and overcame toil and pain by developing labor-saving tools, devices, methods and practices. Further, they improved their welfare by forming beneficial institutions, organizing various societies and establishing educational facilities. With this foundation the early Waller-Dungee ancestors serve as prime examples of entrepreneurship, educational leadership and activism that brought with it the ability to sustain a livelihood that inspires future generations.

Bringing the eye of an industrious, resourceful and craft-skilled family to the record of African American endeavor, the Waller siblings individually chronicle with zest and earnest zeal the essence of the Waller-Dungee allied family footprints following the demise of enslavement.

The Wallers' historical chronicle records the life of a self-taught innovator and patriarch who represents the tenacity of the human, creative spirit even in the face of enormous obstacles. It is as well a story of two families having a strong value system, ingenuity and an inclination to bring social change amid an environment bent on "keeping them in their place." These enterprising efforts bring the social, economic and cultural mores of the African American community during the 19th century and early to mid-decades of the 20th century into focus.

This recollection, wonderfully told in their collective voice, paints an enduring portrait of marginalized residents in the old capital of the Confederacy and its Virginia surroundings. The loving remembrances of ancestors and exceptional parents who survived the turbulent, racist climate of the ugly days of Reconstruction and disenfranchisement are endearing. Coupled with educational empowerment, the Waller-Dungee clan prevailed in this harsh climate and became one of the premier Black families in the capital city of Richmond.

Patricia Carter Sluby, D.H.L., Richmond native

Acknowledgments

We owe a debt of gratitude to several people whose wisdom and encouragement made this book possible. Their input and experience were invaluable in helping us tell the Waller-Dungee story. The entire team rendered exemplary and personalized services and we are indeed grateful. Their efforts made the Waller-Dungee story shine!

Mr. John Wesley Davis, a photographer, met with us at the outset of our project and helped us sort through the hundreds of family photographs that we had collected. He provided information to enable us to tell our story effectively.

Mr. Paul E. Sluby Sr., Esq., a research consultant, specified important aspects to reflect upon as we sought to present our material to form a cohesive and readable document. He viewed our early writings and gave us advice and direction on the myriad factors we needed to consider as we proceeded to write this book. We were pleased to have his significant experience and skill.

The support given by Dr. Patricia Carter Sluby, a registered patent agent, professional genealogist and author, was essential as we pursued our goal of recording the Waller memoir. Dr. Sluby has included our grandfather, Marcellus Carrington Waller Sr., in her book, *The Entrepreneurial Spirit of African American Inventors*. Dr. Sluby's knowledge of the Wallers and the Richmond environment made her an ideal choice to assist us with the book and to write the book's outstanding Foreword.

Mr. Ronnie A. Nichols, consultant, was also instrumental in guiding us in writing our story. Mr. Nichols, a visual artist and historian, is a former director of The Old State House Museum in Little Rock, Arkansas. His editorial advice and research were most beneficial.

Ms. Christine Pride, who is a writer and senior editor and consultant based in New York City, furnished editorial advice that was vital to our completion of this project. She was a godsend who aided us in rewriting our story to make it more appealing.

Further appreciation is extended to Ms. Karen Tobin, whose efforts were invaluable in designing and formatting our book and guiding us through the book's publication process. Ms. Tobin's proficiency, accuracy and timeliness were instrumental in completing our task. We also are grateful for Ms. Shirley Hopkins' formatting expertise.

We acknowledge the significant contribution of Ms. Katherine Pickett, who provided commentary that enabled us to adhere to relevant book publishing standards.

To Mr. Anthony Gary, we express our thanks for his diligence in working with us to design our remarkable book cover. His creativity in depicting three generations was a perfect representation of our beloved forebears.

It has taken the efforts of "a village" to complete this book, and we acknowledge the contributions of its endorsers: the Reverend Dr. Jeremiah A. Wright Jr. and Dr. Hiawatha B. Fountain; and to each one who helped us in any way. We thank God for strength, inspiration and wisdom to prepare this memoir. We give honor and appreciation to those who "lived the story" and bequeathed us such a rich heritage. We pray that God will richly bless and inspire each person who reads our chronicle, to give back to the community and to make a difference in this world.

We give a special acknowledgment to our family, including our brother, Richard Waller, and his wife, Jean; sister Betty Gray and her daughter Leonetty; our late sister Lillian Moore; and our late sister Barbara Nealy, along with her daughters, Ta-Tanisha and Ta-Tianna. They researched family history, provided photographs and shared their stories. We express our thanks to our husbands, LeCount Davis and Aubrey Baden, who deserve much credit for their perseverance while we pursued this dream.

Prologue

We began writing this book a number of years after gathering for a "picture retreat," where we reviewed hundreds of pictures and snapshots of our parents, Richard Alexander Waller Sr. and Florence Dungee Waller, and other kin. It was in September 2011, when four Waller sisters—Jewel, Joyce, Lillian and Betty—along with our sister-in-law, Jean, met for a weekend in Annapolis, Maryland. Sister Betty's daughter, Leonetty, was there also to help her mother and the aunts. Leonetty was a 30-year-old, while the rest of us were "senior citizens," having reached age 65 and above.

We spent a few nights in adjoining rooms at the Country Inn, dined at various restaurants, shopped at nearby outlets and generally had fun being together. But our essential goal was to gather and share important pictures and documents of our kinfolk.

During the years, all six Waller siblings liked to take pictures at various family events, and each of us brought to the retreat our own vast collection of snapshots. We also had photos from the numerous scrapbooks that our cherished mother had left us when she passed away on March 27, 1993, at age 80. Mother was an ardent historian and collector and a civil rights activist. She amassed news clippings about African Americans who were featured in articles appearing in the *Richmond Afro-American* newspaper, *Ebony* and *Jet* magazines and other publications. Her scrapbooks also contained countless letters, cards, photos and other memorabilia.

Jewel, our elder sister, became the custodian of the scrapbooks, and over several years, she had sorted and distributed the pictures and other items in Mother's collection. Eighteen years after Mother's death, the day for sharing our photos had arrived. Once gathered, we examined and organized some 300-plus images, but then none of us wanted to part with any of our own pictures. They were too precious!

Viewing the photographs brought on a range of emotions within each of us. We saw pictures we had never seen before, such as a very formal old photo of an elegant lady in a beautiful long dress. We then turned the picture over and written in faded ink was the name Mary Robinson Williams, our maternal Great-grandmother Mary. We became quiet and reflective. This photo was poignant because of her age when the picture was taken and the knowledge that she had once been enslaved. Seeing her representation was moving and profound. We tried to imagine what Great-grandmother Mary's life was like from her birth in 1852. She must have been strong and had deep faith to endure her difficult circumstances.

We felt much joy seeing our handsome grandfathers' pictures. They were taken when both were young and not yet married and they were two fine-looking men! We could see why our grandmothers would be attracted to them. Our Uncle Fleming Waller's wedding picture was a beautiful image that included all Dad's brothers' families, Grandpa Waller and others. At some point, looking at all of the photos became bittersweet; it was sad that we'd lost so many of these dear relatives, including Dad and Mother. It had been 56 years since Dad had passed away suddenly, and the emotions we felt on that terrible day came flooding back to us.

The image of Grandma Fannie's 1900 sheepskin diploma from the Richmond Colored Normal School gave us chills just thinking of the tremendous sacrifices she must have made to become educated during these times, when her own mother had been enslaved. We felt grateful for Grandmother Fannie's life and its impact and realized that this accomplishment came just 35 years after emancipation.

Grandpa Waller's standing at the display case at the jewelry store he founded in 1900 represented so much courage, perseverance and hope for the future. He was a trailblazer and entrepreneur in Richmond's Black community at the turn of the century. M. C. Waller's jewelry business continues today as Waller & Company Jewelers, and is owned and operated by our brother, Richard Jr., and nephews Richard III and David. After Grandpa Waller's meager beginnings, the company stands strong 120 years later.

These memories gave us the enthusiasm to preserve all the pictures, even though a number of them were aged and in poor condition. We rushed out to a nearby Sam's Store to scan our images to provide, on a compact disc, a set of all the photos for each sibling. This was quite a huge job. We utilized several scanners to accomplish this big task, while other customers waited impatiently for us to finish. After scanning all the images of our parents, grandparents, aunts and uncles, we realized that the hundreds of pictures that we had assembled represented an extensive view of our ancestors' lives. We decided that these images needed to be preserved and our ancestors' stories needed to be told.

The photos from all those years brought to mind our predecessors' strength, resilience, good character and faith in God. Generations of our kinfolk faced challenges and obstacles in a period of blatant racism in Richmond, Virginia, the former capital of the

Confederacy. In spite of the prejudice and bigotry they endured, three generations of Wallers and Dungees persisted and achieved so much. We commend them and highlight their efforts to build a jewelry trade, secure an education and support their families.

Ultimately, they witnessed changes in laws and culture that addressed some of the injustices they and their cohorts had sustained. With confidence, education and faith, our ancestors achieved so much despite tremendous odds. They have left a shining legacy that fills us with gratitude and pride.

Our idea for a Waller Family History book emerged as a result of our reverence for what our forebears had achieved. Passing on this rich history would be vital to preserve and impart links to future generations. We must tell their story; if we don't tell the story, who will? Now in 2020, we are the keepers of the history and the storytellers. Our story must not fade, but be passed on and live on. Our elders were successful and maintained their integrity despite all the obstacles and setbacks they encountered. Surely, we and our offspring can do no less. Now that we, Richard and Florence's children, are the eldest generation, we have also recorded our stories in this book. Several of the same inequities and harsh discriminatory practices encountered during earlier times affected us, as depicted in the stories we share about us since 1938. However, like our parents and grandparents who came before, we were determined, not deterred, and we achieved much success.

The life journeys presented in our "Profiles in Excellence" have been both rewarding and demanding. These challenges are not always recorded with individual chronicles, as we tended to focus on opportunities and successes and not to recount difficulties and impediments. However, each of us or our nuclear families has faced one or more serious trials and tribulations. These included debilitating illnesses, job and housing instability, the emotional trauma of divorce, mourning loved ones, and personal disappointments.

Additionally, there were the day-to-day assaults from a society that, even now in 2020, does not yet fully appreciate and value the potential talent of all of its citizens. Our nation and communities still do not afford the full benefits of "The American Dream" equally to all, and especially not to its citizens of color. Some of the limited remedies initiated to offset this pervasive racism are currently being undone by our government.

It is notable that not one narrative in "Profiles" cites racial discrimination as a reason that one's accomplishments have not been greater or success attained earlier. Discrimination is a very likely factor that limited our achievements and negatively affected our emotional well-being, given the era in which we reached adulthood and entered the world of work. Our group has an exceptionally strong work ethic, after all!

We believe that each Waller member's self-reliance and determination to survive, thrive and overcome all difficulties are reflective of a compelling spirit of endurance that has its deep roots in our religious heritage—the Faith of our Fathers and Mothers. In addition, we were encouraged by our elders to "Always aspire, with God's help, to be the very best that you can be, and do the very best that you can do for God, yourself and others." When you do your best, you can do no more.

We, the children of Richard and Florence Waller, take pride in providing and presenting this history book, *Our Shining Legacy*. We have included accounts of the village in which we were reared and eventful times in our daily lives. May this chronicle serve to document our history for future generations and to motivate all who read our story.

Dedication of this Book of Remembrance: Waller-Dungee Family

This book is dedicated in loving memory of our parents, grandparents, aunts, uncles and all other relatives and ancestors through the ages, on whose shoulders we stand. Their deep faith in God and love of family are principles that sustained and guided their lives. We praise God for them and for the rich heritage they gave us. We keep in special memory our beloved sisters Lillian Waller Moore, who worked with us to develop this book and transitioned December 18, 2018; and Barbara Waller Nealy, who transitioned on May 1, 2020.

To our children, nieces, nephews, grandchildren, grandnieces and grandnephews, and to all those family members who are yet unborn, we leave you this Book of Remembrance, *Our Shining Legacy*.

Prayer of Contrition

This prayer was said, and later sung, at Moore Street Baptist Church each Sunday where four generations of the Waller-Dungee Family worshipped.

'**O** Lord, in love, Thine ear bow down,
O hear Thy people pray;
O may that love that knows no bound
Upon us be today.

'**O** Lord, that humble, contrite heart,
In reverence deep we bring;
Hear Thou the prayer our hearts would pray
The song our hearts would sing.

'**O** Lord, in love, our hearts incline,
To rest upon Thy Word.
O hear, O bless, O save, we pray
Have mercy on us, Lord! Amen.

Words: The Rev. Dr. Gordon Blaine Hancock (1884–1970),
Pastor, Moore Street Baptist Church
Music: Mrs. Pearl Henderson Wood (1914–1998), Organist

In Memoriam
MAY THEY REST in GOD'S PEACE

Evergreen Cemetery, Richmond, VA
Mary Waller Johnson, A, 1897-1931
Bessie Aretha Waller Randolph, A,
    1902-1956
Fleming Waller, U, 1907-1966
Henrietta Winston Waller, GM, 1880-1941
James Clark Waller, U, 1895-1959
Marcellus Carrington Waller Jr., U,
    1899-1973
Marcellus Carrington Waller Sr., GF,
    1873-1957
Nannie Brown Waller, GM, 1872-1917

Forest Lawn Cemetery, Richmond, VA
Jean Waller Brown, C,1938-2017
Barbara Waller Nealy, SS, 1946-2020
Geneva Lee Waller, A, 1911-2002
Marie Carter Waller, A, 1917-1997
Thomas Antonio Waller, U, 1911-1997

Fort Lincoln Cemetery, Brentwood, MD
Conchita Moore, N, 1957-2018
Haywood O. Moore, BL, 1930-2018
Lillian F. R. Waller Moore, SS, 1944-2018
Lopez Moore, N, 1958-2013

Harmony Memorial Park, Hyattsville, MD
Garland Davis, S, 1959-1991

Mount Moriah Baptist Church Cemetery, Victoria, VA
Carla Cousins Waller, N, 1963-2018

Resurrection Cemetery, Clinton, MD
Ronald Thomas, N, 1978-2009

Roosevelt Memorial Park, Chesapeake, VA
Rev. John B. Henderson, U, 1908-1974
Lillian Dungee Henderson, A, 1904-1987
Welton H. Henderson, U, 1912-1976
Frances Dungee Jerome, A, 1910-1989
Reginald Brown Jerome, U, 1902-1986

Washington Mem. Park, Sandston, VA
Carrie Chambers Dungee, A, 1907-1982
Jesse Montague Dungee Jr., U, 1903-1984

Woodland Cemetery, Richmond, VA
Jesse Montague Dungee Sr., GF, 1878-1962
Fannie Williams Dungee, GM, 1878-1943
Lillian Edith Williams Jones, G-A, 1880-1930
Betty Robinson Rowe, GG-A, 1863-1923
Florence Dungee Waller, Mother, 1912-1993
Richard A. Waller Sr., Father, 1908-1955
Mary Robinson Williams, G-GM, 1852-1927

Place of Repose is Unknown
Joseph Brown, G-GF, b. 1839
Betty Booker Brown, G-GM, b. 1845
Benjamin Carter, GGG-GF
Mary Carter, GGG-GM
Elizabeth Collins, GG-GM
William Collins, GG-GF
John Beverly Dean, C, 1930-1999
    Okmulgee, OK
Ethelin Collins Dungee, G-GM, 1849-1929
John Beverly Dungee, G-GF, 1845-1925
Mary Bertha Dungee Lawson, G-A, b. 1885
Joseph Dungee, GG-GF, b. 1818
Rebecca Collins Dungee, GG-GM, b. 1829
Bina Marshall, GGG-GM
Jane Marshall, GGG-GM
Henry Mitchell, GGG-GF
Henry Randolph, U, d. 1982
Isabella Carter Robinson, GG-GM, b. 1822
John Robinson, GG-GF
Benjamin Tuning, GGG-GF
Absalom Waller, GG-GF, 1805-1889
Eliza Mitchell Waller, GG-GM, b.1820
Goldie Lee Waller, A, 1896-1966
Isaac Waller, G-GF
Mary Jane Waller, G-GM, b. 1854
Viola Waller, A, 1905-1907
Virginia Johnson Waller, A, 1921-1987
William Waller, U, b. 1901
Oliver George Williams, G-GF

Legend:
A, Aunt; BL-Brother-in-law; C, Cousin; G-A, Great-aunt; GG-A, 2nd -Great-aunt; GM, Grandmother; G-GM, Great-grandmother; GG-GM, 2nd -Great-grandmother; GGG-GM, 3rd -Great-grandmother; GF, Grandfather; G-GF, Great-grandfather; GG-GF, 2nd -Great-grandfather; GGG-GF, 3rd -Great-grandfather; N, Nephew/Niece; S, Son; SS, Sister; U, Uncle

Part One

Cherishing Our Past

Five Generations of Treasured Waller and Dungee Ancestors

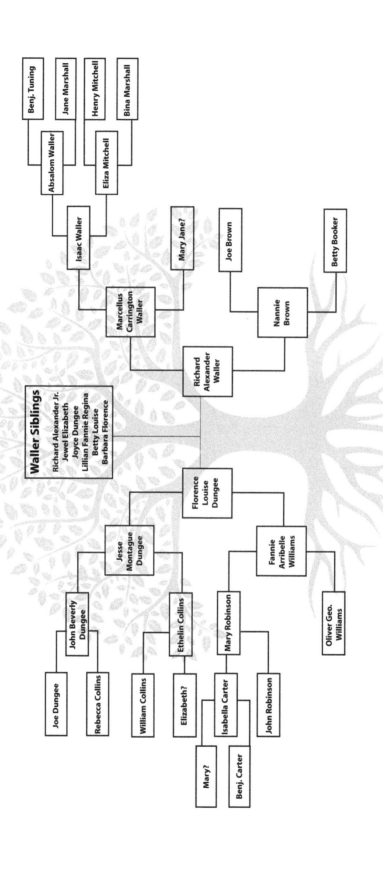

Chapter 1

The Story Begins:

Our Parents, Richard and Florence Waller

**Our parents,
Richard Alexander Waller Sr.
and Florence Dungee Waller**

Daddy, Richard Alexander Waller Sr., was born November 2, 1908, in Richmond, Virginia. He was the son of Marcellus Carrington and Nannie Brown Waller. Grandpa Waller was born in Hewlett, Hanover County, Virginia, and Grandmother Nannie was a native of Cumberland County, Virginia. Grandmother Nannie died in 1917, when Dad, one of nine children of this union, was just eight years old. Fortunately, after a while, Grandpa married Henrietta Winston. According to Dad, she was a caring and kind wife to Grandpa and a loving stepmother to Dad and his siblings. Dad was the middle son of his parents' three youngest children. His younger brother, Uncle Thomas (Tom), and Daddy were devoted to each other through the years. Uncle Fleming was a year older than Daddy; the two of them had a close and loving relationship as well.

Mother, also a Richmonder, was born on May 30, 1912, to Jesse Montague and Fannie Williams Dungee. Grandpa Dungee was a native of

King William County, Virginia. Grandmother Fannie was born in Anacostia, DC. Mother was one of four siblings and was the youngest child.

Both families were longtime active members of Moore Street Missionary Baptist Church on Leigh Street in Richmond. In addition to regularly attending Sunday School and Church services, Daddy and Mother participated in Richmond's Baptist Young People's Union and in other church groups. Both had graduated from Armstrong High School (Daddy in 1927 and Mother in 1929), then studied at Virginia Union University in Richmond for two years.

Subsequent to her college days, Mother renewed her friendship with Oscar, a pal from Virginia Union. He was also a Richmond native. They dated, became engaged and looked forward to their marriage. However, it was not to be. About 1934, Oscar tragically drowned while swimming. The plans for her life with Oscar were destroyed. Mother was sad and grief-stricken.

In the wake of this tragedy, Daddy became a consoling friend and comforter who was determined to lift Mother's spirits and make her smile again. Even though Mother and Daddy knew each other through church and school, they were just friends. Both had moral integrity and were of good character. Mother was beautiful, smart, hardworking and had an affable, gregarious personality. She worked as a housekeeper and with her own mother's kindergarten. Daddy, too, was intelligent and industrious. He was also handsome, enterprising and had a very genial and easygoing demeanor. Daddy was a jeweler and a conscientious businessman whose parents owned properties, as did our mother's parents.

Daddy and Mother found something extraordinary and complementary in each other and began dating. Together, they enjoyed their favorite pastimes, visiting siblings and various relatives, and taking trips to the beach and nearby locales, all the while falling deeper and deeper in love. Before too long they were engaged to be married.

Both Grandpa Waller and Grandpa Dungee were happy about Mother and Daddy's impending marriage. Grandpa Waller and Daddy's stepmother, Henrietta, were pleased that their son had found a suitable wife who was smart and caring and loved him dearly. They knew and respected Mother's parents. Daddy's reputation and personality traits impressed Grandpa Dungee and endeared him to Grandmother Fannie. Grandpa Dungee was confident in Mother's choice of a husband, who was employed and able to provide adequately for his youngest daughter, Florence.

The Waller and the Dungee families were well known and highly regarded in their communities. The Wallers' home was in the Moore Street/Hancock Street area. The Dungees moved to Saint John Street in the historic Jackson Ward before purchasing a residence and returning to live in the West End.

On June 1, 1937, a glorious and blessed day that the Lord had made, Daddy and Mother were joined in holy matrimony. Mother was radiant and looked like a princess with her pretty brown face, keen features with high cheekbones and her slim figure. She was only 25 years old, and quite a "cutie," as her sisters called her through the years. She wore a lovely flowered print dress in a soft pastel shade, her long black hair was adorned with a narrow ribbon and she wore exquisite pearl jewelry, a gift from Dad. Daddy was handsome; about six feet tall, well dressed in a tailored suit enhanced by a print tie and pocket handkerchief. What a good-looking couple.

The wedding ceremony took place at our church, Moore Street, a sizeable and imposing redbrick structure built on Leigh Street by the congregation, after having moved some years earlier from its previous site on Moore Street. The pastor, the Reverend Dr. Gordon B. Hancock, officiated. The sanctuary was very commodious with a balcony, three aisles and scores of pews with seating for several hundred worshippers, and it had a pipe organ. But on June 1, 1937, when our parents wed, only a few relations and friends were present to witness this blessed occasion. Our Grandmother Fannie was not able to attend due to illness. While this was disheartening for Mother, she was not discouraged. Her father, sisters and brother attended. Grandpa Waller and two of Daddy's brothers and their wives were present along with some of the couple's cousins and several close friends. Theirs was a very small wedding, but there was enough joy, happiness and anticipation to fill the sanctuary. When these two amazing families united, Daddy and Mother's marriage brought together a rich heritage of African, Native American and European ancestry.

Our parents did not have to search to find housing. After their marriage, they moved into the upstairs apartment at 723 West Marshall Street in Richmond, in the home owned by Mother's sister Lillian May Dungee Henderson (we called her Aunt May). This elegant brick residence had been owned by our great-aunt Lillie and was inherited by Aunt May. Although there was systemic segregation and racism in the Jim Crow South, Daddy and Mother felt positive that they could survive and even thrive as a couple, and that, they did.

Our Beloved Parents

Mother: sweet, smart, lovely!
Late 1920s

Beloved Daddy

Beautiful young Mother
in the early 1930s

Mother in the
late 1930s

Mother and Daddy,
mid- to late 1930s

Daddy, 1940s

**Mother and Daddy,
1940s**

Daddy, 1950s

**Mother and Daddy in
the park in mid-1950s**

Our parents, early 1950s

**Mother on a winter
day in mid-1950s**

Daddy in the park, mid-1940s

Daddy, early 1950s

Seated: Mesdames Emily Baskerville, Aretha Franklin, Marie Waller, Florence Waller, Margaret Jackson and Thelma Carter. Standing: Matthew Franklin, Thomas Waller, Richard Waller, Clarence Jackson and W. A. Carter, early 1950s.

Chapter 2

Our Grandparents and Their Roots

Grandfather Waller, early 1900s

Our grandfathers, Marcellus Carrington Waller and Jesse Montague Dungee, were born just five years apart, on April 10, 1873, and December 7, 1878, respectively, not long after the Civil War ended. Born in the same era, neither of them received much formal education but were self-taught and had extensive knowledge; we called it "common sense."

Nannie Brown Waller, Henrietta Winston Waller and Fannie Williams Dungee, our grandmothers, would be our grandfathers' greatest assets. Grandpa Waller and Grandpa Dungee were similar in that they were good providers for their families, had long marriages, had established stable accommodations for their wives and families and expected the same of their adult children. They were loyal, faithful mates who took their wedding vows seriously. Both were also loving fathers, determined, hardworking, and honest, and they were men of enormous personal integrity. As Grandpa Dungee said over and over, "Your word is your bond."

Both Waller and Dungee grandparents were able to purchase residences relatively early in marriage. This indicates their ability to plan, save and spend wisely. Our grandmothers were effective homemakers who lovingly nurtured their children and assisted in helping to make their family aspirations a reality. Those hands that "rocked the cradle" instilled bedrock principles: faith in God; love and respect for family, self and others; self-reliance and dignity.

All five grandparents recognized the value of education and encouraged their offspring to obtain as much training as possible. Neither grandfather required any of his children to terminate schooling to help aid younger siblings. Our grandfathers were involved in their progenies' upbringing and continued these close ties throughout adulthood. Their offspring—our parents, aunts and uncles—reflected that upbringing.

Each grandfather had fair skin and looked White. Although our grandfathers' personalities were different, they were similar in their selection of intelligent, beautiful, loving wives with darker skin color. At that time, fairer-skinned members of our race were afforded more status and advantages by both our own and the majority race. Skin color of the children in both the Waller and Dungee clans varied and thus was an unremarkable trait. All relatives were much loved and embraced. For them, and for subsequent generations of kin, skin color has never been an issue when choosing spouses, partners or friends.

While our kin suffered deep disappointments in their lives, many attributable to the discriminatory practices of the day, we are certain with God's help they had the faith and courage to bounce back. They were resilient and found new purpose and anticipation for the future.

Marcellus Carrington Waller Sr. was a leading citizen in Richmond during the period 1900–1940s. His parents died when he was a mere child and he recalled that his mother was Mary Jane Waller, born about 1854, and his father was Isaac Waller. Grandpa Waller was reared by his grandparents, Absalom Waller (1805–1889), and Eliza Mitchell Waller, born about 1820.

Absalom and Eliza were given the opportunity to register their marriage at the end of the Civil War, as provided in the state of Virginia's Cohabitation

Act of 1866. From that registration, we have their parents' names: Absalom's parents were Benjamin Tuning and Jane Marshall. Eliza's parents were Henry Mitchell and Bina Marshall. We have evidence from Hanover County marriage records of 1866 that Grandpa Waller's grand- and great-grandparents were enslaved. Like all enslaved persons in southern states, they were counted as just three-fifths of a person, as a result of the Three-Fifths Compromise of 1790. This legal measure enabled southern states to have more seats in the U.S. House of Representatives.

While a teenager, Marcellus was hired out to work for a household in Hanover County and had no opportunity to secure an education. His entire life, after leaving Hanover County at age 14, was spent working in the Sheep Hill area, now the Carver District of Richmond. At the age of 23, Marcellus married Nannie Brown (1872–1917), daughter of Joseph Brown (b. 1839) and Bettie Booker Brown (b. 1845). Nannie was employed by L. L. Sutherland, a feed dealer for whom Marcellus was also working as a porter.

When their first child, James Clark, was born (1895–1959), they lived at 709 North Second Street. Eight other children were born to this union: Mary (1897–1931); Marcellus Jr. (Junius) (1899–1973); William (b. 1901); Bessie Aretha (1902–1956); Viola (abt.1905–1907); Fleming (1907–1966); Richard (1908–1955); and Thomas (1911–1997). After a lingering illness, Marcellus lost his beloved wife, Nannie, in 1917. At the time, the Wallers resided at 1310 West Moore Street. Marcellus remained a widower for three years and in 1920, he married Henrietta Winston, a native of King William County. She was an agent for the Richmond Beneficial Insurance Company, which was Black-owned. We did not know either Grandmother Nannie (d. 1917) or Grandmother Henrietta (1880–1941).

Grandpa operated a grocery store and established a watch repair business around the turn of the century. He had exceptionally sharp business acumen for a person of his era and circumstances. He thought and planned strategically. Grandpa's name appears in the August 2, 1902, issue of the *Richmond Planet* newspaper, where he is listed in the first group of well-known citizens of the city who immediately purchased stock to fund the American Beneficial

Insurance Company, organized July 28, 1902. The *Richmond Planet* states, "Within 48 hours of Rev. Graham's announcement of the new company, $2,500 was collected from African Americans in the city for the purchase of stock." The *Richmond Times Dispatch* newspaper in October 1918, and again in August 1919, lists Grandpa's purchase of several properties on Leigh Street in its print of Chancery Deeds of Trust. (Now, nearly all years of these historic newspapers are digitized and available for review!)

Grandpa Waller was a religious man who contributed to the business life of Colored Richmond, as well as to Richmond's religious and fraternal circles. He and his beloved wife, Nannie, assisted in organizing Trinity Baptist Church around 1906. In 2006, grandson Richard Jr. formally represented Grandfather and Grandmother Waller at a celebration of Trinity's 100th Anniversary. M. C. Waller worked with the Reverend Marshall Payne in the Mt. Vernon Baptist Church, where Grandpa Waller served as deacon, superintendent of the Sunday School, secretary and treasurer. He later joined Moore Street Baptist Church while it was located on Moore Street. For many years, he taught Sunday School, was assistant superintendent of Sunday School and was a deacon there. He also served as superintendent of the Sunday School at the Afro-American Old Folks Home. Grandpa was an active member of community organizations, including the Knights of Pythias, the Independent Order of St. Luke, the National Ideal Benefit Society and the Magnolia Beneficial Club.

For most of his life, Grandpa Waller was self-employed; he had the freedom of setting his own schedule and priorities. His earnings and economic well-being were dependent upon his own individual efforts and this involved taking risks.

He was always pleasant, congenial and generous, even in his last years when he was not well. We fondly remember visiting him in his expansive bedroom as he sat in a comfortable chair. On September 28, 1957, our beloved Grandpa Waller died. We are grateful for the exceptional legacy he bequeathed to us.

Grandpa Dungee

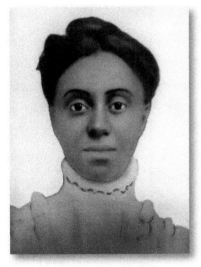

Grandmother Fannie

Jesse Montague Dungee, born December 7, 1878, was the son of John Beverly Dungee (1845–1925) and Ethelin Queen Collins Dungee (1849–1929). They were married in 1875, were distant cousins and were part Native American. Both had ties to the Mattaponi and Pamunkey tribes of the Powhatan Confederacy. Grandpa's paternal grandparents were Joe Dungee (b. 1818) and Rebecca Collins Dungee (b. 1829). All were natives of King William County. We are told that no Dungees were ever born into slavery. Grandpa had six sisters, five of whom died in childhood or infancy. Grandpa Dungee's only sister to survive, Mary Bertha Dungee Lawson, was born in 1885; a homemaker, she married Joshua Lawson and settled in Baltimore.

We understand that Grandpa Dungee resided in New York for a time before returning to Virginia, where he met Grandmother Fannie Aribelle Williams. Grandmother Fannie was born November 16, 1878, in Anacostia, DC. She was the daughter of George Oliver Williams and Mary L. Robinson Williams. Her mother, Mary, was born into slavery in Caroline County, Virginia, about 1852. Great-grandmother Mary had a sister, Bettie Robinson Rowe (1863–1923), who settled in Richmond. It is said that Grandmother Fannie's paternal uncles were basket weavers in Anacostia.

Mary's parents, two of our maternal great-great-grandparents, were John Robinson and Isabelle Carter Robinson. Isabelle, born sometime between 1822 and 1832 in Caroline County, was the daughter of Mary and Ben Carter, who were born in the late 1700s or early 1800s. Isabelle was a midwife who delivered the babies for at least three prominent White families in Richmond: Cliff Weil, Guest, and Wallerstein.

Grandmother Fannie was one of 11 children. She had a number of brothers, one of whom probably was George, who disappeared at age 15 after a circus came to their hometown. However, he did not maintain contact with his mother and siblings and was never seen or heard from again. Some records indicate that George Williams may have settled in Indiana and died in Fort Wayne in October 1932. Several brothers died in infancy. We have no additional information about Grandmother Fannie's father, Oliver, or about any other siblings, except for her sister Lillian Edith Williams Jones (1880–1930).

While growing up, Grandmother Fannie's family comprised her sister, Lillian (Lillie), and her widowed mother, Great-grandmother Mary Williams. Fannie and Lillie were baptized in the Potomac River and were members, as was Great-grandmother, of the Third Baptist Church in Washington. Fannie and Lillie attended Benjamin Banneker School and shopped at the K Street Market in Northwest DC. They moved to Richmond in the late 1890s, joined Moore Street Baptist Church and completed Richmond Colored Normal School. Grandmother Fannie, who finished in 1900, was then employed as a teacher in King William County.

Great-aunt Lillie, we were told, was also a schoolteacher. Her second marriage was to Henry Jones. She left the teaching profession and later became a very successful beautician who owned her residence and operated her business from it. At the time of Great-grandmother Mary's death on September 29, 1927, she lived with our great-aunt at 723 West Marshall Street, in Richmond. Great-grandmother had worked as a housekeeper/domestic.

On June 25, 1902, in Manhattan, New York, our Dungee grandparents married. Grandpa promised Grandmother Fannie that they would return to Virginia if she did not like living in New York. She relocated to Richmond. Around this time, Grandmother Fannie visited Grandpa in New York because he had been hospitalized due to illness. When she arrived, hospital staff could not find him. Grandmother insisted that he was in that hospital. The hospital staff located Grandpa; and because they had identified Grandmother's race, they immediately moved Grandpa from the White ward and placed him in the section for Colored patients. Following his recovery, Grandpa Dungee returned from a brief stay in New York City and was employed by Old Dominion Iron and Steel Works, located on Belle Isle in Richmond.

The marriage of our Dungee grandparents was blessed with four children: Jesse Montague Jr. (1903–1984), Lillian May (1904–1987), Frances Queen (1910–1989) and Florence Louise (1912–1993). The Dungees occupied a home on Jacqueline Street when our mother was born and later moved to St. John Street in Jackson Ward, where Mother attended Baker School.

We were told by Mother that when she was six years of age, the 1918 influenza epidemic affected the Dungees and all of Richmond. Her family members were ill and were cared for by an order of nuns. In Richmond, several schools were converted to hospitals and were used to treat patients during the epidemic. African American patients were treated at Baker School, while Whites were treated at Bellevue School. Grandmother, Mother and her siblings were weak and ill; however, Grandpa Dungee was strong enough to care for all of them for a time. He, too, was impacted by the flu and had to crawl up the stairs to the second floor to bring them sustenance. Mother recalled the horse-drawn carts that came through the neighborhood each day to retrieve the remains of those who had died.

Grandpa Dungee was protective of his wife and children. He and Grandmother Fannie purchased their abode on Lakeview Avenue, which in 1930 had a value of $2,100, a sizeable sum using the standards of that day. They were very well respected throughout Richmond's West End.

Grandpa worked at Old Dominion for nearly 50 years. His challenge was to report for work all the time, on time, and to remain on good terms with his supervisors, who controlled his economic well-being. Due to an accident prior to 1917, Grandpa had only one eye, but was resilient and hardworking and was promoted to foreman. Mother often told us that the boss acquired ideas from our grandpa about how to improve company products and operations, but Grandpa was given little credit for his suggestions and ideas, while "the White boss" received significant recognition for any innovations.

Grandpa reported that he was able to instruct workmen how to manipulate and stack odd-sized and odd-shaped pieces of iron that had been generated by the company, when others could not figure it out! Our grandpa was essential to the business. He had an inordinate spatial ability and could mentally arrange the huge three-dimensional iron parts and quickly understood how they could be stored efficiently, thus saving the enterprise money, time and space. He contributed much to the company's success. Grandpa did not own or drive an automobile; he walked nearly everywhere he needed to go. Most folks did not own cars at that time. His neighbors said that Grandpa Dungee was so methodical that they could set their clocks according to the time he passed their dwellings on his way to work. Responding to his boss's request, when Grandpa was almost 60 years old, he removed a bee's nest and was stung horribly by more than 100 insects. The miracle is that he survived.

During the early 1900s, despite her education and training, Grandmother Fannie, now a married woman, was no longer permitted to teach in public schools. Her teaching career ended with her marriage to Grandpa. To supplement their income, Grandmother Fannie took in laundry, altered clothing and cared for many foster children. Later, she operated a kindergarten from her home. We were told that she prepared delicious fruitcakes when she resided on Lakeview Avenue and even made cakes for neighbors.

Both Grandpa Dungee and Grandmother Fannie were members of Moore Street Church and Grandmother was president of the church's West End Club. Grandpa Dungee was not affiliated with any organizations, except for Moore Street Church.

We discovered that our many Dungee relatives have six different spellings of their name, because census takers through the years spelled the same name differently. These spellings include Dungee, Dunjee, Dunjey, Dungy, Dungey and Dungie. Most have roots in King William County. Grandpa Dungee's uncle, Cornelius Dungee, was the father of our cousin Fred Dungee Sr. (Marian). Fred, his family and his cousin Catherine Dungee resided in Plainfield, New Jersey, during most of their adult lives. Fred and Marian's children are Marcia Dungee Manning (Anthony), who now lives in Richmond, and her brother Fred Dungee Jr., deceased.

Several Dungee cousins have made very significant contributions through the past 150 years. These were Jesse Dungey (1820–1884), state representative of King William County, who served one term in the Virginia House of Delegates (1871–1873); and Shed Dungee (1830–1900), state representative, Buckingham and Cumberland counties, who served two terms in the Viginia House of Delegates (1879–1882). Also, John Riley Dungee, a poet, born 1860 who resided in Norfolk and authored *Random Rhymes*, published in 1929; and Roscoe Dunjee (1883–1965), civil rights leader and legendary editor of the *Black Dispatch*, the first Black newspaper in Oklahoma. In addition, Roger Countee, a noted neurosurgeon in New York City (d. 2001); and Tony Dungy, renowned football coach and author, are part of that group. Of that number, only Tony Dungy (b. 1955) survives.

One of Grandpa Dungee's first cousins, his mother's nephew Simeon Collins, was very fair complexioned. This cousin, Simeon, married a White woman and dwelled in the Fulton area of Richmond. He was a streetcar motorman when Mother was young. Simeon passed for White and had nothing to do with his Negro relatives. We were told by Mother that when our grandpa attempted to visit Simeon and his family, in the 1920s, he was turned away and requested not to visit again.

Grandpa had a wry sense of humor and shared many riddles and stories. He often admonished us with the statement, "Don't take any wooden nickels." It was his tradition in later life to bathe only once each week. We understand this was because he grew up in a time when water had to be brought inside and heated for every bath and for doing laundry and other tasks. Grandpa was thrifty and always looked for a bargain. For example, he purchased seasonal candies and treats at the *end* of the season being celebrated, when it was at bargain prices. Christmas candy was on sale by Valentine's Day and he bought it then! Grandpa's frugality in many aspects of life enabled him to amass funds to purchase a home.

Grandmother's mental and physical health began to fail and she died in September 1943. We were told that she suffered from dementia and diabetes. Our Dungee grandparents had been married for nearly 41 years and had adult children when Grandmother Fannie passed away. Grandpa Dungee was married for the second time in 1944 to Mrs. Emma Lee. After her death in 1951, Grandpa gave up his homestead on Lakeview Avenue and stayed alternately with his son, Jesse Jr., in Richmond, and his daughter, Lillian, in Norfolk. At age 77, in 1955, he married Mrs. Elizabeth Simmons, whom he had met in Norfolk. Grandpa was residing in Norfolk at the time of his demise on May 12, 1962, at age 84, after a long, full, active and happy life. We lovingly think of him and recall his many witticisms and "tall tales."

Our Treasured Grandparents
and Their Roots

"These are they," pastor and officers, honoring the highly efficient and consecrated Chapter Leaders, whose faithful services in cooperation with our loyal and faithful membership, have brought to successful completion Phase 1 of the Greater Moore St. Campaign, May, 1944 Officers of Phrase No. 1, Division Leaders, No' 2, Mrs. Phillis Shark, Mrs. C. A. James Grant, and Assistant Manager, Deacon Andrew J. Williams, Assistant Manager and Leader of Division No. 1. Dr. Gordon B. Hancock, Pastor, Thomas H. Pleasants, General Manager Miss Evelyn Rice, Secretary and Deacon Wm. H. Harris, Treasurer   FOSTER STUDIO

Dr. Gordon B. Hancock, pastor, with officers and leaders of Moore Street Church in 1944. Dr. Hancock, center with cane. M. C. Waller, second row to right of Dr. Hancock.

M. C. Waller with granddaughter Jean at the park, mid- to late 1940s

Family at Moore Street:
Uncle Tom, Mother, Daddy,
Aunt Marie, Grandpa
Waller and Jean holding
bouquet, mid-1940s

Elsie's birthday party:
Betty, Barbara, Elsie and Lillian with
Grandpa Waller, early 1950s

WEST END CLUB

First row, on left,
Grandmother Fannie
Dungee, president of the
Moore Street Church club

Maternal Great-aunt
Lillian Williams Jones

Maternal Great-
grandmother Mary
Robinson Williams

Grandpa's sister,
Great-aunt Mary Bertha
Dungee, early 1900s

Mother and Grandpa,
late 1940s

Mother and
Grandpa, 1950s

Grandpa Dungee,
late 1950s

Our grandparents' home,
1309 Lakeview Avenue

Chapter 3

Our Entrepreneurial Legacy:

M. C. Waller & Sons' First 75 Years

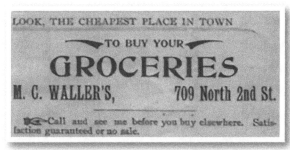

M. C. Waller Grocery ad, 1896 in
***Richmond Planet* newspaper**

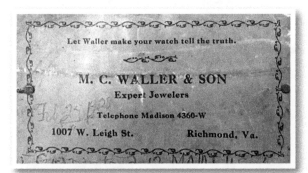

M. C. Waller & Son business card, early 1920s:
"Let Waller make your watch tell the truth."

Grandpa Waller was a pioneer and an astute businessman who had established this eponymous company M. C. Waller in 1900 in Richmond's Sheep Hill district, the first African American–owned store of its kind in the region.

Grandpa Waller's story began in the 1880s at age eight, when he fixed an old mantel clock belonging to his grand-mother. While in his early teens, Grandpa left Hanover County with his Uncle Ben and came to Richmond, securing jobs as a grocery delivery boy and porter. This work prepared him for his first venture, ownership of a grocery store at 709 North Second Street, with his aunt, Mrs. Charity Braxton, as partner. It is said that the grocery store operated from 1895 to 1900.

In the late 1890s and early in the new century, our enterprising grandpa was a trail-blazer among Richmond's Black business leaders. He also was an insurance collector for the Black-owned Richmond Beneficial Insurance Company. Throughout these years, Grandpa Waller collected insurance payments during the day and canvassed for watch and clock repairs at night. By the age of 27, our self-trained grandpa and mechanical genius had opened and operated a grocery store and at the same time, started a jewelry repair company. At its inception, performing watch and clock repairs was its singular focus.

Later, in 1922, Grandpa purchased the property at 1007 West Leigh Street, remodeled it and moved the jewelry repair company to this location, where it functioned exclusively under the name M. C. Waller & Son. A business card from 1928 includes the company's motto: "Let Waller make your watch tell the truth." As his customer base increased, Grandpa could not obtain additional tools and supplies to repair the watches and clocks. Using his tremendous mechanical skills honed as a blacksmith, he made his own tools. There were no wholesale watch and jewelry supply businesses in Richmond, and watch-makers of the other race refused to let him purchase goods from them. Determined and innovative, Grandpa procured old clocks and watches and cannibalized these to secure the parts he needed. Eventually he was able to acquire material from an out-of-town source.

Grandpa taught Dad and Uncles Junius and Tom repair skills, and as a cohesive unit, the four of them managed the business, renamed M. C. Waller & Sons. From the early 1920s through the early 1970s, thousands of customers entered the store on Leigh Street. Houses were located in the block, but our small store was in the middle; houses on both sides were occupied by our grandpa and uncles. The glass storefront and steps to the small glass entrance door were very close to the narrow sidewalk. Patrons entering found an establishment that was alive with the loud ticking of wrist- and pocket watches, and clocks that had been brought in for repair. These watches and clocks were locked away at night, but each morning they were wound by hand; most of the time, there were at least 125 of them. Watches hung by identifying tags; the customer held the other half of the tag and brought it in to claim the repaired item.

The service and display areas of the store were contained in a small but attractive space, probably in a room that was 10 x 25 feet. Uncle Tom, whose workbench was in this front corner, greeted the customers and accepted their items. The showcase, about 10 feet long, held watches and watchbands and also featured a limited selection of sparkling jewelry and gifts. A display cabinet held ink, ink pens and some of the silver-plated articles that were offered. Adjoining the customer area, and separated by a pair of nondescript drapes at its doorway for privacy, was a room of equal size where Dad and Uncle Junius worked. In that section, hundreds of crystals and other watch and jewelry parts were neatly stored and labeled. The store smelled of air freshener, and perhaps jewelry cleaning fluids, metal solder and window cleaner that was used several times a day to keep the glass showcase gleaming.

Closing time at M. C. Waller & Sons was a busy daily occurrence. Jewelry needed to be moved for the night and the showcase covered. All customers' repair items were secured and metal screens covering the window and door required attaching. Of course, the doors were locked. When the 5:30 closing time was near, these nightly activities started. Invariably, on many evenings, a customer or two would come to the door at 5:45 or even 6:00 to retrieve their repair work or purchases being held with a deposit. Daddy and our uncles were skeptical of opening the door at this hour, particularly in the wintertime when it was dark, but prayed that they would be safe and secure and often admitted the customer, thus closing at a later time. Since Uncle Junius lived next door and Uncle Tom did too, for many years before moving, no transportation time was required to return to their families at the end of the workday.

To render even greater service to their large number of patrons in the downtown and East End sections of the city, M. C. Waller & Sons opened Store No. 2 in March 1932 on North First Street under Uncle Junius' leadership. This was a tremendous "leap of faith" to establish another store in the midst of an economic downturn. At this time, the Depression, which began in 1929 was impacting economic markets in the United States and internationally.

The Great Depression undeniably was the worst economic slump in the history of the industrialized world, lasting from 1929 to 1939. It began with the stock market crash of October 1929 that panicked Wall Street and devastated millions of investors. Despite the resulting dearth of consumer spending, widespread unemployment and other economic impacts, Waller & Sons survived.

Eventually, trade at both stores increased and the company weathered the Depression. Uncle Tom attributed the firm's success to "satisfactory work and a constant effort to provide quality service." When Uncle Junius was drafted for military service in 1941, Store No. 2 was closed. After serving the country, Uncle Junius rejoined his father and brothers in the family business and specialized in repairing pocket watches and jewelry. The firm's growth continued. Numbered among the store's dedicated clientele were people of all walks of life and various ethnicities. Some patrons, who came from rural areas in nearby counties, often brought in their own watch or jewelry for repair plus six or eight more watches belonging to friends and neighbors. These customers usually visited the store on Saturday, coming with their shopping bags to hold items purchased during their day shopping in the city.

In the early 1950s, Dad documented a historical account of the family business and stated, "In spite of the handicaps of raising a large family, the lack of proper education and the tedious task of teaching himself the very technical art of watch, clock and jewelry repairing, M. C. Waller had succeeded in accumulating a small fortune, which was mostly in real estate, stock and fixtures." Daddy further wrote, "With his three sons, Marcellus Jr., Richard Alexander, and Thomas Antonio Waller, experts in the trade, M. C. Waller & Sons looked forward to an even greater future in serving Richmond's jewelry repairing needs."

Daddy studied subjects related to commerce and accounting at Virginia Union University. While in college, he competed for and won the title of Fastest and Most Accurate Typist in the city. He utilized this knowledge and these skills to enhance and expand the family enterprise. Watchmaking particularly suited Daddy because he was not able to do physically strenuous tasks. His role in the business was pivotal as he specialized in the repair of ladies' Bulova, Elgin, Hamilton and other watch brands popular at that time. He also engraved clients' watch cases and other items by hand. Uncle Tom repaired smaller ladies' watches, while Uncle Junius was the expert in fixing pocket watches and jewelry. Maintaining the firm's financial records, implementing its operations and innovations, and improving other management functions were also Daddy's responsibilities.

In the early 1950s, Daddy shared his knowledge by teaching a disabled teenager to repair watches. The youth, who was from Chicago, used the skills he learned to create a successful business.

Regrettably, in the prime of his career, Daddy was stricken with cardiac arrest and he passed away suddenly on November 26, 1955.

M. C. Waller & Sons provided quality sales and excellent workmanship, and the company was widely known and esteemed throughout Richmond and the surrounding communities. The firm had the trust of its patrons, who had confidence that the jewelry they purchased was of the quality and value assigned to it. They could depend upon the company's integrity and honesty.

Our much-loved grandpa was in failing health before his death in 1957, at the age of 84. We honor the extraordinary tradition Grandpa established as a true pioneer and great entrepreneur when he founded his business at the turn of the century.

Several years afterward, Uncle Junius experienced health challenges and stepped down from active participation in the business before he passed away in 1973. Thereafter, Uncle Tom retired and closed the shop at 1007 West Leigh Street.

Ring Sizer

Pocket Watches

Watch Strap Gauge

Script Ink for Fountain Pens

Pocket Watch Repair Tools

Jewelry Polishing Stone

Mementos from M. C. Waller & Sons Jewelers at the
1007 West Leigh Street location, 1930s–1950s

M. C. Waller & Sons: The Early Years

M. C. Waller Sr., a distinguished pioneer entrepreneur in the early 1900s

Grandpa Waller, 1940s

Regulator clock repaired by M. C. Waller in 1928

M. C. Waller with showcase, Capital Trade Exhibit, 1934.

Marcellus C. Waller Sr., 1950s

Marcellus C. Waller Jr., 1950s

Richard A. Waller Sr., 1950s

Thomas A. Waller wearing a
jeweler's eye loupe, a small
magnifying glass, 1950s

Richard A. Waller Jr., 1970s

Richard A. Waller Sr. with trophy
from M. C. Waller & Sons presented
to Virginia Union University
basketball star in early 1950s

Uncle Tom in front of
M. C. Waller & Sons
storefront, 1922–1973

M. C. Waller & Sons Jewelers and
the Waller Compound

Part Two

Embracing Childhood

Chapter 4

A Baby Son and a Budding Tribe

Richard Jr., 1939

Daddy went to the family jewelry store reluctantly on a cold day near the end of January 1938. He was anxious because his sweet wife, Florence, our mother, was expecting their first child. She had experienced more than a little discomfort during the night, but had been assured by her physician that there would be a week to 10 days before the baby's arrival. Mother had insisted that she would be fine and that she would phone Daddy if her condition changed in any way. She spent the morning folding and unfolding clothing and diapers for baby-to-be. She arranged and rearranged the few bottles and toiletries that she and Daddy had purchased for the baby. The bassinet that would be baby's bed was ready with soft baby blankets and bibs. Just the week before, they had decided on a name; if it were a son, he would be Richard Jr.; if it were a daughter, her name would be Jewel, their precious gem.

It was ironic that both Daddy and his closest brother, Thomas, were first-time expectant fathers of children who would be born within weeks of each other. Their children would be Grandpa Waller's first grandchildren; although Daddy had five other living siblings, all were childless as of 1938. About 1:00 in the afternoon on January 27, the store's phone rang and it was Mother announcing that she was in labor. Daddy left work immediately to be with her. He drove to their apartment in the car that he and Uncle Tom shared. Daddy then quickly transported Mother to Richmond Community Hospital, which served Black people, where Dr. Zenobia Gilpin delivered their baby, our brother Richard Jr. Dr. Gilpin was married to our Aunt May's brother-in-law, Welton Henderson.

All the aunts, uncles and grandparents adored Richard Jr. He was "the apple of their eyes." After all, he was Richard and Florence's firstborn and the first and only grandson on the Waller side. He was the second Dungee grandson; our cousin John Dean was nine years old at the time. Our Uncle Tom and Aunt Marie's baby girl, Jean Marie, was born just one week later.

Mother and Daddy were enamored of their new baby; they enhanced their parenting skills and learned new ways to make baby Richard content. From the beginning, Richard was known for his hearty appetite. When he was a toddler, Mother left him briefly alone with a cake she'd just baked and frosted, while she went to answer the door. When she returned to the kitchen, Richard had eaten all the chocolate frosting off the cake.

A year after his birth, Mother had a secret. She did not immediately reveal to anyone that she was in "a family way" once again. She felt well and had no discomforting symptoms. She began planning for their new baby. Eventually, it was obvious that she was having another child. Mother and Daddy's siblings and friends were pleased for them. This time, Mother wished for a daughter and she and Daddy had already selected a girl's name. The summer was hot and fall seemed to drag on interminably. Finally, on a perfect day, October 15, 1939, their daughter was born at home on an ironing board, with the help of a midwife, and they named her Jewel Elizabeth. She was the first girl on the Dungee side and was admired by all the kin. Jewel was a precious little baby who hardly cried at all. As a young child she was precocious; when Mother talked with Jewel, the downstairs neighbor, Mrs. Barnes, often thought Mother was talking with another adult. Mother did not talk "baby-talk" to Jewel.

By 1941, the family had moved to their Cary Street home, recognizing that they needed more space for their growing children. Jewel and Richard, ages two and three, no longer needed diapers and it was more feasible for Mother and Daddy to take them to church and to visit friends and relatives. Mother cared for the toddlers each day while Daddy worked; life was serene and pleasant.

When Jewel was three years old, another baby was "quietly" on the way. In preparation for this blessed event, Jewel was taken to Norfolk to stay with Mother's beloved oldest sister, Aunt May, and her husband, Uncle John (the Reverend John B. Henderson). We were told that each night she was at our aunt and uncle's house, Jewel lay on the floor and looked at Mother's and Daddy's pictures, then cried, saying, "I miss my sweet mother and sweet daddy." A short time after these nightly episodes began, Jewel was returned to Richmond to them.

Richard and Jewel were too young to know that a third baby was about to be delivered. They awoke early one morning and did not see Mother; instead they saw Mrs. Moore, a fair-complexioned friendly face with long, reddish brown hair. She was our next-door neighbor who had them in her care while Daddy hurried Mother to the hospital. Joyce, a smiling happy bundle of joy, was born New Year's Eve, 1942. As it was told, the day after her birth, Uncle John and Aunt May visited Mother in the hospital; Uncle John said, "Florence, give me that baby." Mother's response was, "I'm not giving you my baby!" Our parents gave Joyce the middle name Dungee in honor of Mother's parents.

Mother told us that she never mentioned a word to Daddy about any subsequent pending births. "I didn't tell him; he would find out in due time," was her response when we asked her what Daddy said upon learning that they would welcome a new infant yet again. Baby Lillian Fannie Regina, their fourth loving child and third cherished daughter, was born July 8, 1944. She was named to honor our Grandmother Fannie, Aunt Lillian May, and Aunt Frances and her husband, Uncle Reginald. From the beginning, Lillian was a "daddy's girl" who became animated, even as a baby, whenever Daddy walked into the room. Later, in 1946, Mother and Daddy were expecting their household to expand again. It already included Richard, Jewel, Joyce and Lillian.

And then they had twins! April 21, 1946, was a providential day, as our parents welcomed their precious fraternal twin daughters. Betty Louise, the fifth child, was born on Easter at 12:15 a.m. Her twin, Barbara Florence, who was the last of their children, was born at 12:27 a.m. Each daughter was given a part of Mother's name. Everyone adored the two baby girls and their big sister Lillian. When these three were young, Mother purchased similar outfits for them; perhaps they wore the same style dress, or shorts, or coat, but in different colors. On numerous occasions, they were mistaken for triplets. With six babies in eight years, our parents' lives would be full of sacrifice, adventures, experiences and discovery. Ours was a household filled with their love for each other and for us. Each child was unique and would need to have their individual strengths and talents developed. In Mother's own words, "I have six children and they are all different; no two are alike."

At that time, in our community, a family of our size was a rarity. Benefits of our large brood included more camaraderie and joy; we were each other's best friends and playmates, and we had hugely fun-filled lives. We were the center of our parents' universe, which consisted of faith, immeasurable love and discipline.

Our Family Won This Contest!

Baby Contest at Gilpin Court, 1946.
Mother (center) with Barbara while Daddy holds Betty.
Lillian, Jewel and Richard gather beside Mother.

The Way We Were

Richard Jr., 1939

Richard, Mother and Daddy, 1938

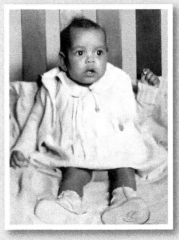

Jewel, 1940

Lillian, 1948

Joyce, 1944

Betty and
Barbara, 1946

Barbara and Betty, 1948

Betty and Barbara, 1948

A popular event for children in the 1950s was a Tom Thumb wedding. Lillian, on the left end, and Betty and Barbara are part of the group.

Tom Thumb wedding at Moore Street Baptist Church in the late 1940s.
Bride and Groom: Wilbur Dyer and Kathy Dyer
First row from left: 2nd, Elsie Waller; 4th, Lillian Waller; Second row from left:
2nd, Joanna Toney; 3rd, Jean Marie Waller; 4th, Alease Payne; Third row from left:
5th, Joyce Waller; 7th, Richard Waller; Third row: 1st on the right, Jewel Waller

Chapter 5

Memories of Cary Street

**Richard in front of our Cary
Street home, 1952**

Our home at 1222 West Cary Street, though modest, was a beautiful castle of joy and love that was safe and secure for us. We lived there for about 13 years, beginning in 1941. Purchasing it represented a major milestone; an accomplishment that was gratifying to Mother, Daddy and their kin. Our family of eight—our parents and eventually the six of us—was not financially affluent, but was rich in character, spirit and faith. According to our parents and other family members, these were the essential ideals needed to shape our lives.

This house was an ongoing hub of activity from morning until night. Beginning with her marriage in 1937 until 1952, when she reopened her kindergarten, Mother was not employed. With six children, her days were filled with everyday duties. Dad's rather limited income from the family business and gifts from relatives were sufficient to maintain us and provide for some extras. Daddy was able to supply Mother with periodic domestic help, as well as funds for her personal spending and family contingencies. Mother made breakfast and sent us off to school before beginning her household tasks; she also cooked and performed a myriad of other functions. Almost every day, she was busy laundering loads of clothes in a top-loading automatic washer, hanging them on the line in the back yard and ironing. Even during this time, in the early 1950s, most neighbors did not own an automatic washer, but we were fortunate to own one. Grocery shopping was nearly a daily routine and Richard accompanied Mother to carry the groceries in his wagon.

Our section of Cary Street in the West End was similar to various Black neighborhoods throughout the city of Richmond. The area was mostly residential with a variety of commercial interests here and there. Even our block housed a small upholstery establishment and a meat market. Families with children occupied most of the places of residence, and the adults held various types of jobs. Among the hardworking adults were schoolteachers, nurses, postal workers, domestic workers and owners or co-owners of small enterprises—just like Dad. Our street was not different from the overall community, as people from all walks of life were our neighbors.

The two-story semidetached white frame house had a small porch and a postage stamp–size front yard with a fence and gate. Our back yard was somewhat larger. Upstairs, there were initially only two bedrooms, but Daddy divided the larger one so that Richard could have his own small bedroom and all the girls shared the remaining space. With a bunk bed and a double bed to accommodate all the girls, there was not much space left. Putting a dresser, a chair and a utility cabinet along with the beds in this room was a challenge, and it was hard to keep the room neat, but we did. Big sister Jewel slept on the top bunk and little sisters delighted in kicking her mattress just to annoy her. Another troublesome activity was the little sisters' finding a way to unlock Jewel's cabinet where she stored her lipstick, crafts, letters and other items.

A favorite part of the house was the breakfast room, which had a large table. This was a good-size space situated between the dining room and the kitchen; it led to our only lavatory and a side door, which we used to access the back yard. Richard, Jewel and the others spent hours at the table studying, doing homework and playing board games. Our chosen game was Monopoly, and sometimes we played the game until late at night. We tried to buy up all the structures on Park Place, the Boardwalk, and other expensive properties, while avoiding "going to jail" or "back to GO."

It was here in our Cary Street home that we experienced a traumatic incident. Wednesday, June 13, 1951, seemed to be just an ordinary day, though cloudy with darkening skies, and Mother was busy with household tasks. When she last had checked on Lillian, Betty and Barbara, they were playing outside in our front yard. Unexpectedly, for a few minutes, Mother heard sounds as if a freight train were nearby. Then an extremely loud crash came from the front of the house. She rushed to investigate. Even though it had turned very dark in the middle of the afternoon and started to rain, Mother did not realize that a tornado had torn through the section of Richmond where we resided.

Mother saw that our house had been smacked by a huge telephone pole. It had hurtled through our living room window and was extended inside for about four feet. In addition, our roof had been peeled back by the wind, and in some sections, she could see the sky; rainwater was pouring in and was damaging the upstairs bedrooms. More frightening to her was the tin roof lying in our front yard, which had blown off of a neighboring residence. With some trepidation, Mother approached the porch looking for her three youngest children and did not see them. Lillian was almost seven and the twins had just turned five. Were her twins and Lillian playing out front or had they gone to visit neighbors before this roof crashed into the yard? She prayed for their safety and began screaming their names. Where were Jewel and Richard? Mother was thankful that she herself was not in the living room and that she had not suffered any injuries, but where were her children? Her heart was racing. Oh my God, she thought; Lillian, Betty and Barbara are under that roof.

In minutes, fronts of apartments nearby had been peeled away and one could look at some buildings and see all the rooms inside. Everything inside was exposed, just as you see in a doll house. Now, unsettling questions raced through Mother's mind, but most importantly, where were the children? She prayed out loud, "Lord have mercy! Please keep my children safe!"

At that very moment as she was bending down to look under the roof, Daddy drove up with their four daughters in the car. Mother was not aware that Daddy had returned early from work. He had driven Jewel and our three younger sisters with him for a quick ride to a grocery store that was close by. Mother was nearly overcome with joy, thankfulness and relief. "Thank you, God!" she said; her girls and husband were out of harm's way! But where was Richard Jr.?

Within the next few minutes, Richard came into view with his friend Clarence Jackson. Richard, who was 13 years old, was delivering newspapers with Clarence when the tornado began. At some point during the storm, they were standing outside a residence, which afforded some protection, when the owner beckoned to them and sheltered them indoors.

It was a blessing from God that none of us was under that rooftop, as Mother feared. Even though our place was damaged, we were all unharmed. Daddy was so thankful that Mother and all of us were safe, and he had some regrets that Mother had been alone and was frantic with worry about their children's safety. Daddy was perturbed at the severity of damage to our house.

Our parents were not aware of a tornado warning. This was an F3 tornado, which by definition has winds between 158 and 206 miles per hour. In its wake, the tornado injured dozens of people, destroyed 100 domiciles and damaged more than 1,000 houses and buildings in Richmond. It was particularly earth-shattering in our sector of the West End.

Mother thought about the future and what would happen to her youngsters now that the house had suffered extensive damage? Where would her girls and boy sleep? She didn't know where she and Daddy would sleep, since their bedroom was in the front, which suffered significant damage. Where would the funds come from and how long would the repairs take? Where would the children study and prepare their homework? How would she do laundry and cook the family's meals?

The next day, the local Red Cross placed a waterproof tarp over our roof and we were able to remain at our place as renovations were made. Fortunately, insurance covered most of the cost of repairs and our property was eventually restored. Our parents were grateful for our safety and for help from the Red Cross.

Chapter 6

Joyce's Temporary Visit to Norfolk

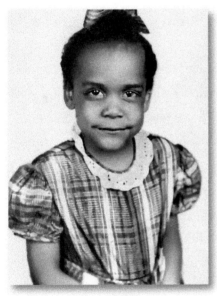

Joyce, 1948

At age three, in 1946, Joyce went to Norfolk to live temporarily. Aunt May, an elementary school teacher, and Uncle John, pastor of Bank Street Baptist Church, were a childless couple. They thought that Mother and Daddy would benefit from having Joyce stay in Norfolk for a few months, as the twins, born in April, and Lillian, age two, required nonstop care.

The months turned into years and all concerned had adapted to this temporary arrangement turned long term. Joyce had become the Hendersons' "foster daughter" and the three of them were a close and loving family. When Joyce turned six, Aunt May enrolled her in Norfolk Public Schools.

Aunt May and Uncle John showered Joyce with affection and attention and she loved them too. Aunt May provided the necessary discipline; Joyce had a very strong will. Their household was a loving and secure place, as was our Richmond home. Aunt May was determined not to overly indulge Joyce just because she was the only child in their household. Joyce was assigned chores and learned early to accept a few responsibilities.

She had a large bedroom and lots of books and toys. Joyce accompanied Aunt May or Uncle John nearly everywhere it was feasible. This included club and church meetings, conferences, concerts and more. The Bank Street Church congregation embraced Joyce as the Hendersons' daughter and a "Preacher's Kid," or "P.K." Many were educators; they stressed the value of education and encouraged all of the church youth to plan for college. Several of these members were professors at Norfolk State and could furnish essential information. The church provided scholarship funds for its youth. Aunt May and Uncle John quietly donated additional monies to students in need.

A variety of people came to the Henderson domicile, next door to the church, with requests for financial and other assistance. On one occasion, Uncle John was out of the city and Joyce, then age eleven, admitted a stranger. He was a tailor of men's clothing and made a lewd comment to Aunt May: "Let me drape my tape around your shape." Joyce was frightened, but Aunt May was not intimidated. He left very quickly after Aunt May lifted a heavy wooden chair from the floor, pointed it in his direction and told him what the result was likely to be if he did not get out!

Christian faith and social justice, as embraced by Bank Street Church and exemplified by Aunt May and Uncle John, made a tremendous impact on Joyce's life. When they hosted visiting ministers, missionaries or any other guests, Joyce was usually the only youth present and was included at the adult dinner table and in some discussions. She mostly listened intently and tried to absorb what was being discussed.

Aunt May ensured that Joyce had a variety of experiences in addition to church services and events. Joyce had piano and dance lessons and was a Girl Scout. Aunt May frequently hosted Joyce's friends. On Saturdays in the fall, the family attended Historically Black Colleges and Universities (HBCU) football games. Joyce had no interest in the sport and begged to be left in the car to read and sleep; her parents did not acquiesce to her requests. Joyce sat in the bleachers and read. Was *nerd* a word yet? Alvina Gramby was a close pal who participated in church youth activities with Joyce. Lelia Hinton and Joyce were friends who frequently attended school basketball games and other events together. Joyce was a "big sister" to Muriel Cauthen, who was a close neighbor.

Sometimes on Sunday afternoons, Uncle John would serve as guest preacher at any one of the numerous small country churches near Norfolk. If there were a repast at the church, usually the food was just the best, especially the scrumptious homemade cakes! The restrooms (outhouses) were the worst, though! When the honorarium was collected for his service as guest preacher, Uncle John always gave it back to the church. After one of these occasions, when she was about age seven, Joyce commented, "Uncle John needs to go somewhere and get a job before we starve to death!"

Joyce did not question the arrangement that took her away from Mother, Daddy and her siblings; after all, she had lived with Aunt May and Uncle John, who were her loving Norfolk parents, from age three. She traveled to Richmond often to visit. In addition, our parents and we siblings frequently visited Aunt May, Uncle John and Joyce. On their many train trips to Norfolk, Richard and Jewel listened to the conductor announcing in a booming voice, the various stops: Petersburg, Waverly, Wakefield, Suffolk, Norfolk!

Family rhythms with Aunt May and Uncle John were determined by church worship and activities. Joyce's participation at Bank Street Church never felt onerous. She loved the church family and was a member of the Sunday School and all other church-related youth organizations. She could hardly wait for Bank Street's Annual Youth Week, when the youth were apprenticed to the pastor, deacons and others.

Joyce was a part of the Henderson household and, by extension, was regarded as a granddaughter by Uncle John's parents and a niece by his siblings. She graduated from high school in 1959 and enrolled at Norfolk State. During Joyce's junior year at Norfolk State, our sister Lill went to Norfolk to complete high school and she graduated from Booker T. Washington High in 1962. She and Joyce, who were only 18 months apart in age, got along extraordinarily well. They went shopping, attended school sports events and spent time with friends. It was a precious and wonderful time, as Joyce now had a sister to share secrets with, who resided under the same roof; sometimes they talked or watched television all night.

Aunt May and Uncle John loved Joyce unconditionally, and they provided a plethora of inspirational, educational, cultural and fun activities for her. She misses all four parents' wonderful loving presence. She is thankful to all of them for their love and profound impact upon her life.

Chapter 7

Sundays Were Special

Moore Street Baptist Church, Richmond

On Sunday mornings, the radio was tuned to a gospel music station and we listened to some of Daddy's favorite music sung by the Five Blind Boys of Alabama and Richmond's own Harmonizing Four. After a quick breakfast, usually cereal and toast, or muffins Daddy prepared, we headed to Sunday School, walking about a mile from Cary Street through streets occupied by White residents. We were ages seven to fifteen. We did not walk together as a group, but walked individually or maybe in twos, separated by a block or so. Jewel and Richard, who left for church first, looked back repeatedly and walked slowly to ensure the safety of their younger siblings. Our parents could rely on Jewel and Richard to make certain that the younger sisters were safe.

Early in our lives, we were taught that the Sabbath was holy and to revere it. Each of us confessed our faith when we were quite young and all except for Joyce were baptized at Moore Street Church by the Reverend Dr. Gordon B. Hancock. Mother and Daddy witnessed all of these baptisms in various years; for Richard and Jewel, on the same Sunday in 1948; for Lillian, 1954; and on Easter in 1955 for Betty and Barbara. Joyce was baptized by Uncle John at Bank Street Baptist Church in Norfolk in 1948. Our parents insisted that each meal begin with a grace and at night, we said our prayers. We learned Bible verses and recited them at the Sunday dinner table. At times, a sibling humorously quoted the shortest verse, "Jesus wept." Mother and Daddy informally expressed their faith and gratitude to God on a daily basis and reminded us that God loved us and all other people equally.

Each Sunday School session, held in the basement of the church, began with children's prayers and spirited songs of faith we liked to sing, including "Jesus Loves Me." Sometimes Jewel played piano for the Sunday School's closing session. When we were older, we were involved in various church groups, including the Junior Usher Board where Mother served as advisor, the Baptist Young People's Training Union and the Junior Choir.

Our planning for Sunday started early in the week when our special church outfits, "good clothes," were laundered and readied. For some unexplained reason, socks and ribbons for Lillian, Betty and Barbara to wear to church could never be located from one week to the next. More had to be purchased; almost every Saturday, we walked to the nearby Kennedy's Variety Store at Cary and Morris Streets or to the Five and Ten Cents Store at Lombardy and Main Streets to buy socks and ribbons. The stores must have made a fortune from the Wallers' repeated purchases! On Saturdays our kitchen became a mini hair salon where the younger sisters' hair was washed and pressed with a hot comb that Mother heated on the stove. She had countless talents and styling hair was among them. Our hair had to be just right for Sunday. Jewel's help was required; she usually shampooed hair while mother pressed and curled. The kitchen was extremely hot during this process. It was an effort to keep still while one's hair was being pressed and curled, to avoid a painful burn from a hot comb or curling iron. We still suffered some burns, in spite of Mother's caution.

After Sunday School, we all visited Grandpa Waller and our uncles and aunts who inhabited adjoining houses a few blocks from the church. Uncle Tom and Aunt Marie, Uncle Clark and Aunt Goldie, and Uncle Junius and Aunt Geneva resided at 947, 949 and 1009, surrounding the jewelry store at 1007 West Leigh Street. This was the Waller compound. Grandpa Waller and the aunts and uncles seemed delighted to have us come by. Each household blessed us with a few coins after learning of our progress in school and encouraging us to do well. A pharmacy that sold sweets and other goodies was located nearby, and we stopped in to buy candy, spending some of the change we had just been given.

When Lillian, Betty and Barbara received money at the Waller compound, if it were a dollar bill to be divided among the three of them, the born mathematician, Betty, would make sure that the money was divided evenly. The dollar was broken and each obtained $.33. Then they purchased bubblegum that costs one penny for three pieces and each had a piece.

We returned to church in time for the worship service and met Mother and Daddy. Mother was a member of the Willing Worker's Usher Board and once each month, this group ushered. The 25 or 30 women on the Usher Board were very impressive, dressing alike, greeting worshippers and marching down the aisles in precision to pass the collection plates. These ladies were well organized and took their ushering responsibilities seriously. They met monthly and sometimes Mother hosted Usher Board meetings. Also, Mother was among a few ladies on the committee who selected their uniforms. One uniform Mother helped select was a lovely navy blue tailored dress with a white collar, which was attractive on all the members. Mother always looked forward to the fourth Sunday when she ushered.

Daddy and Mother dressed in their Sunday best. They looked stunning. Mother's hair was always beautifully styled and she wore her favorite perfume, Evening in Paris, which was popular at the time. Mother was regal, forever attired in a pretty dress or suit. In winter, her coats were accented with fur, or she wore a little fox fur around her shoulders for warmth. Daddy looked elegant in a well-tailored suit. They were thrifty shoppers and budgeted their funds well. They learned this skill early as the parents of six.

After service, we returned home and it was time for dinner. Our meal consisted of Mother's delicious fried chicken, macaroni and cheese, green beans and our favorite, corn pudding, all of which she had prepared before leaving for church. Occasionally on Sundays, Mother invited a friend or two for dinner. Not a morsel of food was ever wasted. It was Jewel's job to set the table. More than once, Jewel needed to locate a tablecloth, iron it and then put it on the table.

Following dinner, we went for a pleasurable car ride with our parents. Usually Daddy drove us to Byrd Park to feed the ducks; during the preceding week, we had saved all the heels from loaves of bread in order to have food for the ducks. The younger sisters played and enjoyed climbing up and rolling down the hill surrounding the reservoir, then we went to Dairy Queen for ice cream. Disputes arose about who would sit beside the car window on the trip to Dairy Queen. On other Sunday afternoons, we visited our grandfathers. We rode to Belle Isle to see Grandpa Dungee, where he worked at this time as a watchman. Frequently, we returned with our parents to visit Grandpa Waller and other Waller kin in the Waller compound. Jewel played piano for them. On occasion, we dropped in to see our Uncle Buddy and Aunt Carrie. These Sundays were chock-full of activities for the entire day. By evening, we were exhausted and did not object to going to bed.

A beautiful Sunday afternoon in the park. Mother, Barbara, Lillian, Betty and Daddy, late 1940s

Barbara, Lillian and Betty on Easter, about 1950

Chapter 8

Family Time in the Waller Household

**Jewel, Richard, Lillian, Mother,
Barbara and Betty, early 1950s**

In 1954, Mother and Daddy bought a spacious brick home at 2108 Rosewood Avenue in an established and well-kept community with tree-lined streets in the West End near Byrd Park. This community was newly accessible for African American ownership, as residences became available due to "White flight." The house had four bedrooms, a sunroom, a full bathroom, a powder room on the first level and also one in the basement. It provided plenty of space for Mother, Daddy and the six of us. This two-story house had a large porch, where Mother could sit and chat with the neighbors. She could also place her flowerboxes there and plant colorful, abundant petunias each year.

Prior to our move, Daddy and Mother visited this property, which had "good bones" but had not been kept in pristine condition. Daddy promised to make the house a "palace" for Mother. All of us were excited about moving to a new residence; we were involved in the initial cleanup effort and did whatever we were asked to do. After the house was emptied of debris, repairs made, walls painted and floors refinished, Mother's "palace" was ready! On the day of the move, Mother was working temporarily in a beauty salon to supplement Daddy's income for extras needed in the new place. Jewel had been collecting part of our allowances for a while so that we could purchase a special gift for our parents to let them know how much our breathtaking new home meant to us. We decorated their bedroom with a satiny blue and pink comforter, throw rugs, and a matching trash can. We prepared the rest of the house and put the furnishings and most items in place. Daddy and Mother were nearly overcome with elation to see their new bedroom decor and their homestead in good order when they returned from work.

There were two discrete groups of us children at our home in September 1954. Three of our sisters, Lillian, Betty and Barbara, were enrolled at West End Elementary School and were at least five years younger than Richard and Jewel, who were sophomores at Maggie Walker High School. Mother still managed to interact with both schools' PTAs. Joyce, who was in Norfolk, was in seventh grade.

Lillian, Betty and Barbara were eager to attend their new school, which was only a block from our address. This school was formerly John B. Cary, but a new school had been built for White students and the building was now designated West End Elementary, a school for Colored children.

The younger girls were enthusiastic about living near Byrd Park, where Daddy and Mother had taken us on Sundays through the years. Now, the park was just three blocks from our door and walking there was a favorite activity for them. Occasionally during the summer, our adventuresome sisters Lillian, Betty and Barbara packed their lunch and blankets in a wagon, walked beyond Byrd Park to Maymont Park and spent the day relaxing under a huge magnolia tree. When they were age eight or nine, they appeared on a WTVR Channel 6 show called "Ranch House Tales," a live program for children that was televised locally. Betty and her sisters were thrilled about appearing on TV and wore cute cowgirl outfits for the production. No doubt three African American sisters participating in a television show in Richmond was a unique event for those times.

These three sisters were young entrepreneurs and environmentalists; from age 12, they delivered the *Richmond Afro-American* newspaper and *Ebony* and *Jet* magazines; and sometimes babysat for families living nearby. They also searched the streets in our vicinity for bottles and returned the bottles for cash. A small soda bottle was worth two cents; a large one was worth five cents. Every penny added up.

Some days, Lillian, Betty and Barbara walked downtown and shopped for doll baby clothes from Troy's, Murphy's, Grants and other stores. One particular year for Christmas, they all wanted skates along with a 52-game variety chest and made it clear to everyone in the family. On Christmas morning, under the tree were three pairs of skates and three 52-game variety chests! Later Christmas Day, they visited Aunt Carrie and Uncle Buddy and under their tree were three more pairs of skates and three more 52-game variety chests for them. They had enough to skate and play games all year.

Until Lill enrolled in junior high school, she, Betty and Barbara did most things together. They played games incessantly, including jack rocks, pick-up sticks, jump rope and red light, and rode their bikes. Mrs. Ellison, a musician, gave them piano lessons. Betty and Barbara, who had been in the same classroom through elementary school, finally were separated when they reached junior high, and they had different teachers from then on. Both of them played violin in junior high school but this was not their interest and they did not continue beyond one year of instruction.

Each of our three younger sisters had a distinct personality and expressed her individuality. At an early age, Betty demonstrated interest and proficiency in mathematics. By age five, she knew her multiplication tables up to 25 times 25, and asked Daddy, "How far does it go?" When she was very young, she found six puppies, brought them to our place, thinking a puppy per child, but soon learned subtraction as we could keep only one puppy in our home. She was introspective and studious and liked challenges: games, puzzles and problem-solving. She won several contests sponsored by the *Richmond Afro-American*.

Barbara was fond of reading and was talkative and outgoing. She truly was a "Miss Congeniality." In addition, she adored pretty clothing and had a sense of fashion by the time she reached her teenage years. She, Betty and Lillian habitually walked from our home on Cary Street to the jewelry store. Barbara displayed an early interest in jewelry and other beautiful things. When she visited the store, Daddy, Uncle Junius and Uncle Tom gave her gifts of gold and silver jewelry and her first watch. Barbara also walked to High's Ice Cream Store, which was located near our home, and purchased a pint of ice cream for 15 cents; a price unheard of today. *Archie* and *Jughead* comic books were some of Barbara's favorite reading materials as a child. She continued her interest in reading throughout her adolescent and high school years; one of her beloved books was *The Diary of Anne Frank*.

Our sister Lillian, on the other hand, was interested in the healing arts. She always showed compassion for others and liked caring for people. At about age seven, she loved to play "doctor," enlisting Betty and Barbara as her patients. Lillian pretended to give Betty medicine using a sewing needle to prick her finger. Lill applied this medical interest when visiting Mrs. Ella Foster, a neighbor and member of Moore Street Church, who had sustained severe burns in a house fire. Lill visited regularly and massaged Mrs. Foster's painful skin. As Lill grew older, she was especially considerate of anyone in our home who did not feel well and prepared food for them and offered consoling company.

Lill was industrious and found jobs babysitting neighborhood children. However, she did more than babysit; if there were dishes in the sink, she would wash them and do other light chores—sweeping, wiping up countertops and so on—while she was in their abode, exhibiting a passion for things to be clean and neat. Perhaps she already had made the connection between cleanliness and health. Lillian liked to cook when she was quite young, and Mother allowed her full range of the kitchen. She enjoyed baking cakes and other goodies; Barbara was the tester and she ate anything Lill prepared. Lillian was fond of reading the Bobbsey Twins series and everything she could about the human body. Our cousin Elsie and Lillian were unusually close; she regularly visited Elsie and they walked together from Elsie's home to the dime stores downtown to browse and shop.

Our Uncle Buddy and his wife, Aunt Carrie, resided near us and were our closest Dungee relatives in the city. They took a particular interest in Lill, probably because Lill aspired to become a nurse and Aunt Carrie was a nurse. On occasion, they took Lill on vacation with them to West Virginia. She visited with them a lot more than the rest of us siblings did. She took walks with Uncle Buddy and Aunt Carrie through the nearby cemetery, and whiled away many afternoons sitting on their porch listening to their stories.

We nearly can taste the delicious cakes that Uncle Buddy and Aunt Carrie sent to each of us every year on our birthdays! It was quite a scene in our neighborhood when a big truck from Thalhimer's Department Store Bakery came to our address several times a year to deliver a beautifully decorated custom-made cake. What a blessing and great childhood memory.

The Virginia Museum of Fine Arts was perhaps a mile walk from our residence and Lillian and Joyce visited often during the summers and holidays. They were fascinated by the Egyptian mummy exhibit. Other times, they attended theatrical and musical performances at Dogwood Dell, an outdoor theater in Byrd Park. The sisters were thrilled that neither of these facilities was a segregated venue, and both were open to all. When Joyce came to Richmond, she had a great time as part of the "Waller pack." We did not decorate the Christmas tree until Joyce arrived.

Jewel was "Mother's helper," the big sister who kept things in order when Mother participated in various meetings and community events. As a young girl, Jewel delighted in reading mysteries, writing to pen pals, baking cupcakes and playing with friends. Jewel spent much time with cousin Jean. They were members of the same Girl Scout troop and were together repeatedly, taking piano lessons or sitting beside each other in church on Sundays. Jewel was a babysitter for several families in the neighborhood and relished making a few dollars. She was caring and generous and developed a sense of style, a perception she gained from her role models, Mother and Aunt May.

A key pastime for Richard in his preteen years was playing with the toy soldiers he collected. He had obtained an extensive collection over the years and reveled in placing soldiers in various formations, lining them up on a table in his small room. The younger siblings delighted in knocking down all of Richard's soldiers, which annoyed him to no end. No one ever claimed responsibility for this, and he never retaliated.

Richard liked playing outdoors with his friends, particularly Charles "Puffy" Brown, who lived around the corner from our Cary Street abode. He spent so much time at the Browns' place with Puffy and his brothers that one may have thought Richard was one of the Browns' sons. Puffy's parents had six boys and only two girls; our family had all these girls and only one boy. A large open field was behind our house and the Browns' home, and Richard and Puffy played there for hours on end—building forts, playing hide-and-seek and other games, and just having fun. Sixty-five years later, Jewel can still hear Mother's voice calling "Richard Jr., come on home to dinner!" One day after digging a fort, he fell into the hole and badly cut his knee; a scar remains to this day.

Some of Richard's other chums were Thars Baskerville, Clarence Jackson and Clarence Lee. These four on occasion went to a nearby ballfield to watch baseball games. Mr. Lee, Clarence's father, owned a small restaurant just around the corner from our house, where we visited almost daily for snacks. Richard regularly purchased his favorite soft drink, Tiny's Grape Soda.

Daddy and Mother were good friends with the parents of Thars Baskerville and Clarence Jackson. Both the Baskervilles and the Jacksons had daughters who were Jewel's age. So, the families all spent much time together. Jewel and Richard also played ball and rode bikes with pals and other teenagers living in the vicinity. Summer evenings expended at Clark Springs playground; meeting with pals at Stell's Shell, a small restaurant patronized by teenagers; and visiting classmates in Brookfield Gardens on Sunday afternoons were preferred activities during Richard and Jewel's teenage years. One memorable annual event was the Easter Monday picnic at Bryan Park. Most of their buddies from school and the neighborhood came with picnic lunches and all had a grand time eating, listening to music and playing sports and games.

Whenever Joyce visited, Mother wanted her time at home to be pleasurable and insisted that Jewel take her to parties, because Joyce had few good friends in the city. "Where are you going that you can't take your sister?" was the question Mother asked Jewel. Of course, Joyce went along with Jewel, in spite of lagging behind her by three years in age.

Jewel socialized with her friends, especially members of The Charmerettes, a girls' social club. Mother and her peers, Mrs. Baskerville and Mrs. Jackson, helped to organize the club around 1953. Mother requested a young schoolteacher, Miss L. Barbara McDaniel, to be the group's sponsor; she was a wonderful leader and role model for the teenage girls. Nessa Baskerville, Cynthia Jackson, Shirley Jefferson and Iris Knight were among Jewel's close pals who were members of The Charmerettes. They learned charm and etiquette, performed community service projects and sponsored a wonderful gala every year. All the girls donned beautiful long dresses for the lovely event and members invited their special date and other friends to attend. At the time, clubs for many of Richmond's Black teenage girls were popular. Among them were The Gay Misses, of which cousin Jean was a member, and The Little Women.

Most of the girls in The Gay Misses and The Little Women resided in the city's Northside, as did some of Richard and Jewel's classmates. Like the Byrd Park section of the West End where we moved, this community had been in transition due to White flight, and Black people were purchasing the spacious brick houses now available for sale to our people. The large two-story properties had wide porches and sizeable back yards and were purchased by numbers of Richmond's prominent professionals. Cousin Jean and her parents moved from their Leigh Street address to a lovely home in Northside. Thus,

Richard and Jewel were regularly invited to the social events given by their friends who lived in this section of the city.

Richard and Jewel, in addition to finishing school homework assignments, completing household chores and working at M. C. Waller & Sons, were occupied with all of these activities and others common for their age. Among additional happenings that kept them busy were attending football games and other sports events; holiday gatherings and parties with chums; church youth events; and parties in our back yard or basement.

Daddy and Mother encouraged Richard and Jewel to invite their high school pals to visit at our place. When Jewel and Richard had parties, our parents were always around for these hosted events and kept a very close eye on the goings-on. Pretty colored light-bulbs, plentiful snacks and sodas, and of course dancing to popular rhythm and blues music provided for a fun-filled environment. Their get-togethers were held during their junior and senior years in high school. These would be some of the last times they spent with many of their childhood friends and classmates. After graduation, a number of their friends relocated, joined the military, sought employment or enrolled in colleges out of the city.

Lillian, Richard, Betty, Mother, Daddy, Barbara and Jewel, 1950s

Chapter 9

Living in Segregated Richmond

Betty's sign with mementos from the March on Washington, 1963

While our childhoods may have been fortunate and idyllic, we still experienced the cruel hand of racism. In segregated Richmond, we were living in a culture that diminished the humanity of African Americans and made it such that realizing the American Dream did not seem possible for us. We could not expect fairness or equal treatment from the White majority, whether in business interests, the courts or other institutions in Richmond. This culture was composed of two separate entities: the White community and the Black community. Except for minimal interactions, such as contact with salespersons in the stores, bus drivers and city employees, Whites and Blacks had few opportunities to connect and learn about each other and relate on a personal basis.

This discrimination, which had been reinforced by laws, gave birth to a vibrant group of African American entrepreneurs. In the 1940s and '50s, when we were growing up, we were aware of a thriving community of African American–owned businesses in the city's Jackson Ward and in other parts of the city. These businesses served a special need and treated Negroes with respect and dignity. Among such

Black-owned institutions were the *Richmond Afro-American* newspaper and Consolidated Bank. The bank was founded by pioneer Maggie L. Walker, a role model and an inspiration for Black entrepreneurs. She devoted her life to civil rights advancement, economic empowerment and educational opportunities for Jim Crow–era African American men and women. Black professionals and Black-owned insurance companies, as well as numerous restaurants, hotels, mortuaries, grocery stores, drugstores and other establishments, were entities our family and most Blacks supported.

Also notable was Richmond Community Hospital, which served Blacks and was opened in 1903 on the campus of Virginia Union University. The hospital was cofounded by Dr. Sarah Garland Jones, the first woman certified to practice medicine by the Virginia State Board of Medicine, and her husband, Dr. Miles Berkley Jones, both African Americans. St. Philip Hospital, a separate hospital for Black people, was a component of the Medical College of Virginia. St. Philip had a reputation as the hospital for Blacks that was used to train doctors of the majority race.

The racism and the inequities we encountered occurred systematically. Tax-supported facilities such as City Hall, the public libraries and public waiting rooms were designated as being for "Whites only" or "Colored only." We sat in the "Colored only" section of Richmond's Broad Street Train Station, not in the larger, cleaner, conveniently located general Waiting Room. Public libraries were not available to us; we could use the Rosa Bowser Library, but not the main Richmond Public Library. Segregation in Richmond during our childhoods meant, among other things, that we had to ride in the back of the bus and other transportation. Although Black residents were taxpayers in the city of Richmond, local, state and national laws denied Black citizens equal access in both the private and public domains. Facilities were separate and unequivocally unequal.

While downtown shopping, we could not sit and eat when we visited the store's restaurants. In instances where we could buy food, we had to stand or carry the food off of the premises. Certain retailers did not allow customers of our race to try on clothing and hats. Many of these firms were heavily patronized by Black customers, and even this collection of establishments did not treat all its customers fairly. Employment opportunities were severely limited for our race at these companies. Jobs as cooks and janitors were the abundant employment options for Blacks in downtown department stores. For Black college-educated women, teaching was a popular profession along with nursing. Most Black college-trained men worked in the U.S. Post Office, as "white collar" employment in other concerns was unavailable for them.

In this environment, we all experienced our share of pervasive racism and segregation on a daily basis. At age five or six, Betty boarded a city bus with Mother, Barbara and Lillian. Betty and our sisters sat on the long front seat behind the driver. The bus operator then asked Mother, "Are those your children? Get them to the back where they belong." That incident greatly impacted Betty and though she was only a small child, she felt the anger and animosity in the driver's voice and resented the way he spoke to Mother. Even now, Betty avoids riding in the back of a bus.

Another time, as Mother put money in the bus fare box, Jewel sat on an aisle seat in the second or third row beside a White man who quickly brushed his hand toward her, as if brushing away crumbs. His action made Jewel feel sad and rejected. Mother took Jewel's hand as she passed and they walked together to the back of the bus.

Richmond schools also were segregated. We walked past Whites-only schools to reach our schools for Black students, where the buildings needed repairs and the furnishings, equipment and books were well used and no longer good enough for White students. However, our teachers, part of our "village," were excellent educators who were caring and urged us to study ardently and to love learning. The outstanding academic preparation we received from them, albeit in inferior school buildings, has served us well throughout our lives. Following the May 17, 1954, Supreme Court ruling that outlawed segregated public schools, Prince Edward County, Virginia's schools, among others, closed rather than integrate. Richmond schools continued to be segregated. However, in 1970, students were bused to achieve racial integration. Teaching staffs had been desegregated a few years earlier.

When Mother confronted racism and discrimination in her everyday life, she pushed back hard. Store clerks were always corrected when they did not call Mother, "Mrs. Waller." In fact, her store account information was in Daddy's name, "Mrs. Richard Waller," because she did not want the clerks to know her first name and call her Florence. Mrs. Waller demanded respect. While downtown shopping, Mother was met with prejudice almost every time. Once, she was not allowed to try on hats while shopping at Thalhimers Department Store. As a result, Mother cut up her charge card and ceased shopping there. To this day, Betty retains the cut-up charge card.

Frequently, Jewel went shopping with Mother and observed that when Mother was tired and wanted to buy a snack, usually hot dogs and sodas, she could make her purchase, but could not sit down at a table or booth to eat, since all seating was reserved for Whites. This was devastating for Mother and very painful for Jewel to witness. If we needed to use the restroom or wanted a drink of water, we experienced these same indignities, as we found our way to the lower level and rear of the store to the "Colored" restrooms and water fountains. Restrooms were often identified for "Colored Women" or for "White Ladies."

As a young child, Joyce had attended performances designed for children at the Norfolk Arena. Blacks were admitted, but could only be seated in the balcony. In the early 1960s, Joyce, who then was a Norfolk State College student, joined a group of other students who protested segregation at a movie theater on Norfolk's Granby Street. At the time, the Virginia State Legislature was determining the funding for its public colleges and universities. Norfolk State College protesters were asked to curtail their protests while funding was under discussion; of course, they did not!

Joyce heard stories of Aunt May's encounters with racism years earlier while teaching in Richmond and then in Norfolk. In 1938, like other Black teachers in Virginia, Aunt May was paid a good deal less than White teachers whose academic credentials and teaching assignments were similar to hers. Attorney Thurgood Marshall, who later became a Supreme Court Justice, was instrumental in the fight for equal pay for Black teachers in Virginia. While pastor of Bank Street Church, Uncle John was very active in the fight for racial equality in Norfolk and throughout the state. In the days following his appearance before a Norfolk City Council meeting to give the opening prayer, he received death threats. He was unafraid, but Aunt May and Joyce were terrified for his safety.

In Richmond, after the end of Jim Crow, municipal pools were closed rather than admit Blacks. As a ten-year-old, Barbara had a great interest in learning to swim and anticipated swimming in the pool at Byrd Park, but the city dismantled the pool to circumvent integration, thus preventing anyone from swimming there. During Richard and Jewel's early years, there was only one swimming pool for Black people in the city of Richmond. Richard learned to swim; however, the pool was very crowded with youngsters from all over the city.

Barbara participated in the sit-ins and other activities protesting discrimination. She and additional youth activists marched to the Lowe's Theater in downtown Richmond.

The movie tickets were bought by a friend who could "pass" for White. The person at the theater who took the tickets said, "They don't serve n———s here," and the protesters left peacefully. The group also went to Murphy's or Woolworth's stores and were told that they could buy food, but would not be seated; they might stand up and eat or go upstairs, which at that time had seating available for Blacks.

Richard was riding a city bus to high school one day with his classmate and good friend, Tyrone Gresham. After boarding, the two sat on the long seat behind the driver. Usually, Whites sat in these seats. When two White people embarked the bus, they wanted these seats, but Richard and Tyrone did not move to vacant seats in the rear. The driver stated "these n———s won't move," and then called the police. Richard, Tyrone and all Black students on the bus were made to leave the bus and they needed to walk the remaining blocks to their usual stop near school.

After Jewel graduated from Virginia Union and just before she left Richmond for employment in New York, she had the opportunity to interview for a secretary's position in a large Richmond firm. However, Jewel remained in New York for only a few months. After returning to Richmond, she inquired about the secretary's job, but was told that there were no jobs available. Had she been hired for this position, she would have been the first Black secretary in a major company in the city.

The injustices we experienced on an ongoing basis certainly raised our consciousness of the prejudice and second-class citizenship we all withstood. But we kept our heads high, trusted God and developed confidence in ourselves and our abilities. Our parents and other relatives and members of our "village" were superb role models. While we were denied opportunities, we were not daunted. We were inspired by the fortitude, endurance and faith in God that Mother, Daddy and other ancestors exhibited during difficult times. They overcame and we will too!

In spite of all of the prejudice we bore day to day, Mother did her share to help make the dream of equal opportunity become a reality for her children, our cohorts and coming generations. One facet of Mother's life's mission was to work for societal change and for empowerment of the African American community, and she was involved in civil rights activism during her entire adult life.

Part Three

Celebrating a Multitalented Mother

Chapter 10

A Phenomenal Woman–Parent, Teacher, Civic Activist and More

Mother had a very full and satisfying life. She truly was a phenomenal woman. It is difficult for us to comprehend and describe how she accomplished so much through the years.

In her late teens, the 1930 census indicates that Mother worked as a cook in a private residence in Windsor Farms, an exclusive "Whites only" area of Richmond. She was enrolled at Virginia Union University for two years but was forced to drop out during the Great Depression. Her studies in early education there established the academic foundation for her career as kindergarten and nursery school owner and teacher.

In 1935, following in the footsteps of her mother, she opened a private kindergarten in the dwelling she shared with her parents on Lakeview Avenue. In years prior to that time, Mother had assisted Grandmother Fannie in operating a nursery school at our grandmother's home. Mother reactivated her own kindergarten in 1952, when our youngest sisters were six and eight years old and had begun public school.

Grandmother suffered a debilitating illness for six years before she died in 1943. However, despite her illness, toddlers Richard and Jewel were placed in her care for very short periods when Mother stopped in to visit. During these times, Grandmother Fannie read to them. Mother was so close to Grandmother that she did not attend church on any Mother's Day, following Grandmother Fannie's death. The emotional toll of Mother's bereavement was exacerbated on that day. It was traditional at Moore Street Church that if your mother were alive, you wore a red flower; if she were not, you wore a white flower. This exhibit of loss was just too painful for her.

Mother was very bright, loving, caring and cheerful. For her, the glass was always more than "half full." Her outlook on life was consistently positive. She loved Daddy dearly and loved us dearly. And, most importantly, she was a dedicated, wonderful, tireless Mother, and with six children, that was not easy. Mother and Daddy had that kind of loving marriage that made an ideal environment for our happy and pleasant childhoods and eventual success as adults. Our home life was relaxed; Mother was not a housekeeping fanatic. We children were permitted to enjoy our home in spite of the spills, scuffs, finger-prints, disorder and other superficial damage that occurred day to day. Loving discipline was a central facet of our upbringing. We were instructed to be obedient and respectful and to behave all the time, but particularly when we were in the care of others or out in the community. Misbehavior was not tolerated. Appropriate punishment was meted out when we disobeyed our parents' rules. Punishment might be denial of a privilege, an infrequent actual spanking or being excluded from the family group and sent to bed.

The activities Mother provided for us expanded our horizons and exposed us to a variety of situations, people, communities and challenges. We were exuberant at those times we visited Daddy's cousin, Mr. Harry Thomas, who owned a restaurant at First and Leigh Streets in Richmond. Mr. Harry opened the restaurant just for us on Sunday, when it was normally closed. We reveled in sitting at the counter and having the Thomas cousins serve us milkshakes and ice cream. The weekend train trips to Norfolk, annual outings to the beach with Moore Street Church, Fourth of July picnics, and excursions to the Virginia State Fair, which required taking three different buses, all fostered new learning and were exciting, though Daddy was often unable to indulge in these adventures due to his frail health.

Mother was ever-present to assist us as we grew older and became even more involved in our numerous endeavors. We knew that our homeroom was likely to obtain more credit for parent participation because Mother attended all PTA meetings. Whether we were participating in Tom Thumb weddings, involved in Hi-Y activities or attending Charmerettes Christmas parties, we could always depend on Mother to be in attendance.

Whatever the situation, Mother lent a hand to a neighbor in need. She was the person who collected for a floral memorial spray, food, money or other expressions of care and concern from the neighborhood. She knew how to delegate and usually designated one of us to perform the task of going house to house to collect funds for one of those purposes, and there was always a positive response from residents who were canvassed.

Reciting poetry at church and home "teas" and other venues was an activity that gave Mother great satisfaction. Two of the poems she often delivered are printed in this book.

Our mother was very well thought of and well known in the area. She appreciated everybody and everybody appreciated her. Mother saw virtues in individuals and looked for good behavior and wholesome character. She chose her friends on the basis of their character; her friendships were not predicated upon one's educational level or economic success. Mother instilled these ideals in all of us. We were taught to treat everyone with respect and dignity. These values have stuck with us and have stood the test of time, now that we have reached three score and ten years of age.

Mother was never reluctant to accept a leadership position in parent-teacher organizations, her church and civic groups throughout the city of Richmond. Mother was always available to volunteer and was enthusiastic about making a positive difference, regardless of her role. She was able to coordinate all of these outside undertakings with her immense home responsibilities; she had Daddy's loving approval and backing.

Mother organized the West End School Parent-Teacher Association and was elected its first president in 1954. An additional example of her parent activism included petitioning the Richmond School Board when plans were being made to redraw enrollment boundaries for Armstrong High School. With the new boundaries, Richard and Jewel could not attend Armstrong, where our parents had graduated. Maggie L. Walker, the school where they were assigned to attend, had the reputation for admitting veterans and other older students. The Richmond School Board did not change its policy regarding the boundaries. Though the parents' group was met with opposition from the school board, their voices were heard in committee testimony. Both Richard and Jewel and their peers from the West End had no choice and enrolled at Walker in 1953. Three years later, students in the class of 1956 became the first Maggie Walker graduates to attend college in record numbers and achieved great success.

Through her acts of kindness, volunteerism, courage, concern, grace and with a critical intellect, Mother made a very positive difference in her neighborhood and its schools and culture. In our early years, Mother had a variety of involvements in civic and community endeavors. When Richard and Jewel were quite young, in the 1940s, Mother took them to a small building on Jacqueline Street to attend meetings of a civic group. She was thoroughly invested in the work and efforts of the Richmond Crusade for Voters and the local branch of the National Association for the Advancement of Colored People (NAACP). In addition, she was a member of the Delver Woman's Club Civic Affairs Interest Group and other community groups. Mother's civic activism included participation in campaigns to register voters, eliminate Virginia's poll tax and encourage citizens to vote.

She represented the Richmond Branch, NAACP, at numerous state and national conferences. On some occasions when Mother traveled to these conferences, Aunt May came up from Norfolk and stayed with us. From time to time, Mother solicited our help with her civic affairs duties. While he was only 10 or 12 years old, before one election, Richard and a friend encouraged voter turnout on Clay Street, where Black residents were settled, by going door to door.

Mother was a firm believer in supporting the city's Black-owned businesses. She often patronized such restaurants, grocery stores, dry cleaners and suppliers of fuel and household products. She utilized the services provided by home improvement and maintenance contractors in our race as much as she could.

In 1963, Mother sponsored a bus for transportation so we and others in the community could attend the now historic 1963 March on Washington. Barbara and Betty heard Dr. Martin Luther King Jr. give the famous "I Have a Dream" speech. Joyce also attended the march, traveling from Norfolk with Uncle John and several church congregants.

The recipient of many honors and awards throughout the years for her work, dedication and leadership, Mother was awarded a certificate from President Harry S. Truman in 1948 for her community involvement and from the NAACP. Mother treasured letters she received from two civil rights icons. In 1963, she received a missive from Dr. Wyatt

Tee Walker recognizing her effort in securing full access to the John Marshall Hotel for the Southern Christian Leadership Conference held in Richmond. A letter from Dr. Martin Luther King Jr. declining an invitation she made on behalf of the Delver Woman's Club in 1964 to speak in Richmond, was among Mother's cherished mementos.

Through her work operating a home-based kindergarten on both Cary Street and Rosewood Avenue from 1952 to 1963, Mother was afforded the opportunity to develop and mold numerous young minds. Her kindergarten students received the same preparation for life that she gave us, her children! She taught them to be respectful, kind and honest and to help each other. They learned their alphabets, numbers, colors, how to write their names and to recite the Lord's Prayer, Bible passages and poems. By the time they were old enough to attend school, most of her pupils could read.

Mother also provided daycare for some children whose parents worked. They arrived at our home well before 7:30 a.m. and left about 6:30 that evening. Her weekly fee was $3.00 to attend kindergarten and $5.00 for those who stayed all day. Annually, she sponsored a bus excursion for her charges and their parents to the Washington Zoological Park. Mother was valued by her students and parents alike and very many area parents were anxious to place their little ones in Mother's care. She worked diligently and patiently with her three- and four-year-old learners, preparing them for that big day when they entered public schools. Here are excerpts from letters from former kindergarten pupils:

> I remember our lessons in the basement where we went over every letter sound, nursery rhyme, and number we could count to. When I went to school, I was more than ready and had been given a head start because of Mrs. Waller's teachings. I did well in most all areas and was put in honors classes in high school and a special self-study pilot program in college. Mrs. Waller was a member of my church and I never missed an opportunity to speak to her and tell her thank you for helping me get my start. What a great mentor and sweet lady she was. I will always be thankful for her being in my life and for all I learned from her.

Camille Walker Spain, December 2018

I will remember your mother most importantly as my first teacher. She helped me build a strong foundation for education and nurtured my love for learning. She helped me open the world through the doors of books; how to create, imagine and dream. I remember Mrs. Waller as a fiercely independent Black Woman. She seemed to be afraid of NOTHING. I "took" Mrs. Waller in my heart with me to elementary school to read a book to the principal and was admitted at age 4. I "carried" Mrs. Waller with me to college and graduated on the Dean's List. I thank God for her love, for her life.

Beverly Brown, March 1993. Kindergarten Class of 1956

These letters attest to Mother's motivation and inspiration.

**Mother and her kindergarten class, 1953.
Beverly Brown is on the first row, sixth from the
left. Mother is on the front row, at the far right.**

Beverly Brown (inset)

Part Four

Suffering a Major Loss

Chapter 11

A Time of Despair

**Mother, Daddy,
Barbara, Lillian and Betty**

It was 1955 and our parents' dreams were starting to come true. Life was busy for all of us. Mother was occupied with parent-teacher organizations, church and kindergarten; Daddy was working relentlessly at the jewelry store, exploring new ways to build the firm and to reach and serve new customers.

On November 26, our family attended the Armstrong-Walker Classic football game. Richard and Jewel were seniors at Walker and because Jewel's boyfriend was on the football team, our family wanted to lend its support. This was an annual rivalry between the two local Black high schools, a popular event among Richmond residents and a fun tradition. At the time, Lillian was in Norfolk visiting Joyce, and Jewel went to the game with friends. Our parents and our twin sisters, who were only nine years old, enjoyed the event. Following the game, Richard was driving home with Daddy, Mother, Betty and Barbara. Just a block from our house, Daddy was stricken with a fatal heart attack. He collapsed, slumped over on Richard's shoulder and his life ended. An ambulance was called, but medical personnel could not reverse his condition.

Jewel had just arrived home when she heard someone screaming on an adjacent street. She walked to the corner to see Mother crying, screaming and being consoled by neighbors. Mother yelled and yelled, "Your daddy is dead!! Your daddy is dead!!" His untimely death from this medical crisis at age 47 was an overwhelming loss for Mother, for the six of us and for all of our kindred. This day was a tragic one that we have never forgotten.

Daddy had a heart disorder, which apparently resulted from his severe reaction to poisonous stings from a caterpillar when he was much younger. The stings weakened his heart. But none of us children was aware that Daddy's heart complaint was so serious. We knew that he saw the cardiologist regularly and took medication daily. Sometimes Richard accompanied Daddy to this White doctor's office on Grace Street, near our store on Leigh Street. At the time, no Black cardiologist practiced in the city of Richmond. Daddy also needed to rest in the evenings after work, and his physical activity was limited. He had specific dietary constraints too: he ate lamb, which we children ordinarily did not eat; we ate pork. However, when we saw Daddy with lamb chops and other special foods, for example, we always asked for some of his food and he consistently shared it with us.

He was an extremely devoted husband, a caring and fun-loving father, who only used discipline as a very last resort. On those occasions when a spanking was needed to reinforce disciplinary measures, Mother was the one with the strength for this task, not Daddy because of his fragile health. Daddy taught Richard to drive and gave all of us his good advice and guidance. One day when Richard was wrestling with us, Daddy reprimanded Richard and said, "These are your sisters; they are ladies. Treat them royally."

Daddy was a dedicated son and brother and a lifelong, faithful member of Moore Street Church. He had a wonderful personality and a quiet, reserved and pleasant demeanor. Everyone liked our dad. Lillian described Daddy as her best friend. Jewel played his preferred hymns, "In the Garden" and "The Old Rugged Cross," on the piano in our living room. A favorite pastime for Daddy was playing cards with good friends Clarence Jackson, Matthew Franklin and others. He and Mother also enjoyed visiting relatives and socializing with friends from the community and the church.

Daddy was able to enjoy living in our "palace" at 2108 Rosewood Avenue for a little more than a year before passing away. Even though our family lived in a new neighborhood, all the community embraced us and was saddened by the news of Daddy's sudden demise. This was the era when black crepe fabric was hung on the door to notify friends that there had been a death in the dwelling. As was customary, Daddy's remains were brought to our home to lie in state for several days before the funeral service. It was especially devastating for us children to see our daddy lying in a casket in our living room, looking so lifelike but not alive. Mourners visited Mother and us all day and into the late evening. There were so many of them and some were tearful. Seeing them brought a repeated awareness of our great loss. Our daddy had gone too soon.

We thank God for allowing Mother to live for another 37 years after Daddy's death. We also thank God for the wonderful years Dad was with us and for leaving us countless cherished memories.

I used to dream about a girl
Who'd be so very sweet,
Who'd be so dear and lovable
She'd sweep me off my feet,
I dreamed she'd be so thoughtful
And so wonderful to me--
But you are still more perfect
Than I ever dreamed you'd be!

With love
Richard

Keepsake Mother's Day card from Daddy to Mother, early 1950s

A Tribute to Daddy and His Favorite Hymns

In Loving Memory
Dad

He never looked for praises
He was never one to boast
He just went on quietly working
For the ones he loved the most.

His dreams were seldom spoken
His wants were very few
And most of the time his worries
Went unspoken too.

He was there... A firm foundation
Through all our storms of life
A sturdy hand to hold on to
In times of stress and strife.

A true friend we could turn to
When times were good or bad
One of our greatest blessings
The man that we called Dad.

IN THE GARDEN

I come to the garden alone
While the dew is still on the roses
And the voice I hear falling on my ear
The Son of God discloses.

And He walks with me,
    and He talks with me,
And He tells me I am His own;
And the joy we share as we tarry there,
None other has ever known.

THE OLD RUGGED CROSS

On a hill far away, stood
    an old rugged Cross
The emblem of suff'ring and shame
And I love that old Cross where
    the dearest and best
For a world of lost sinners was slain

So I'll cherish the old rugged Cross
Till my trophies at last I lay down
I will cling to the old rugged Cross
And exchange it some day for a crown.

Chapter 12

Mother Endures and Sees Us Through

Our Rosewood Avenue home, 1954–1993

Somehow Mother endured the horrific loss of her beloved husband of only 19 years. It was by the grace of God that Mother's deep faith sustained her and gave her the strength to carry on. Our Waller and Dungee grandfathers, uncles and aunts rallied around Mother and us and tried to provide stability and comfort. Although greatly grieved, the six of us did what we could to assist Mother as she consoled us and helped us deal with the sudden loss of Dad and to adjust to life without him. We all remained on our best behavior, despite our feelings of loss and anger. We children wanted Daddy back.

Our first Christmas without Daddy was an abysmal holiday. We did not feel like celebrating; our emotions were in shreds. Both Aunt May and Aunt Frances came back to Richmond that Christmastime to offer their encouragement and brought lots of presents and treats for us. It still was hard to feel anything but sadness. In the months following Daddy's death, on Sunday afternoons, we visited the cemetery where Daddy was interred. The emptiness pervaded every aspect of our home life.

In her grief, Mother was unable to prepare all the meals and perform the household tasks as she had done previously. We sometimes purchased prepared food. Grocery shopping was minimized; she was not up to undertaking so very many household responsibilities alone. Mother, with Aunt May's help, learned to handle challenging financial matters, which Daddy had always managed. The family income from Daddy's employment had dried up, but Social Security benefits gave Mother a small amount that she could count on.

Previously, Daddy had driven Mother and the family as needed. The loss of Daddy motivated Mother to attempt to learn to drive. Jewel was instructing her on a sunny Sunday afternoon while they were at the cemetery when Mother ran up over a curb and could not return the car to the roadway; they called for help. Mother was discouraged by that experience and never tried to drive again. She depended on Richard and Jewel to take her and the younger sisters to church and other places.

While in elementary school, Jewel was advanced to Richard's academic level and the two of them continued at the same grade through high school. Richard and Jewel had to focus closely on events surrounding their graduation, which was in June 1956, just seven months after Daddy passed away. Mother was drawn into their graduation planning, and their maturity and academic success gave her a measure of comfort. "Daddy would have been so proud," she often said. Mother and other relatives were thrilled to see Richard and Jewel walk across the stage and receive their diplomas.

We children had difficulty adjusting to our changed lives without Daddy, but we persevered. Richard felt that he had to be the "man of the house," and he believed that he had responsibility for our mother and for ensuring his sisters' welfare. Richard assumed that he would begin working in the family business after graduating, and he did. Jewel wanted to attend college and was apprehensive about her ability to afford it. She continued working at the family business, received a small stipend from the college and later began working in the college business office during her sophomore year. Joyce felt the loss keenly, but because she lived in Norfolk and had Uncle John as her second father, its impact was less traumatic. Lillian was severely crushed by Daddy's death, as he and Lill were extremely close and had a special bond. Adapting to his death was more challenging and took an extended period of time for her. Betty and Barbara were too young, at age nine, to fully grasp the severity of their loss. Mother's involvement in their school, church and other activities was diminished. They could no longer participate in their Brownie Troop because Mother could not pay for their uniforms.

As time passed, Mother gradually regained her ebullient personality and was the warm and cheerful Mother we knew. She was able to resume her kindergarten, day care and other activities and commitments. Spending time with family and friends was important to Mother. Her renewed zest for life led her to organize a club of her many close friends who rallied around her. All were interested in losing weight and named themselves the "Topettes" (taking off pounds). Mother enjoyed her membership in the club and playing her favorite game, Pokeno. Periodically she hosted Topettes meetings in our home. Mother continued her work with civic and church organizations, attending local and out-of-town meetings and conferences. After the early passing of our dad, it was even more important for Mother to witness advances in civil rights and racial equality in hopes that we would develop self-reliance and be afforded equal opportunities to achieve future success.

In 1959, Mother was briefly married to a minister, whom she knew from her years at Virginia Union. This gentleman, who was pastor of two churches near Richmond, was widowed but had no children. At times, Mother and the younger girls visited these churches for Sunday services. We believe his marriage to Mother, who had six children, required critical adjustments that he was unable to make. Their marriage was not successful and was soon dissolved.

During this period, we were all busy with work, academic pursuits and various school and church organizations. From 1956 through 1964, all six siblings completed high school. Joyce in 1959 and Lillian in 1962 graduated from Booker T. Washington High in Norfolk. Betty and Barbara graduated from Maggie Walker in 1964. Mother was there for us, guiding us and sharing her wisdom as we faced these years of many challenges and opportunities. She was an ardent supporter in all of these efforts and we know that Daddy would have been full of pride for each one's accomplishments.

In 1964, Mother moved to Washington where three of her daughters had relocated for employment. Eventually, Mother was hired by the Nursery School of Bethlehem Baptist Church in Southeast Washington. Earlier, she had held a position at a firm in downtown Washington. Mother resided in the District for two years, then returned to Richmond in 1966 and worked for a year or so as a dormitory director at Virginia Union. It was here that she met Mrs. Rallene Hanson, also a dormitory director. Mother next accepted a position as director of Mosby Memorial Baptist Church's day care center around 1968. Following her service there, she retired from this vocation.

She joined Mrs. Hanson, an officer in Eta Phi Beta Sorority, Inc., in chartering a chapter in Richmond, Alpha Delta. Mother held numerous leadership positions, including that of Eastern Regional Director. In 1973, she was honored by Eta Phi Beta for her service and contributions to the sorority. Many tributes were given to Mother, including an expressive poem, "A Tribute to Our Mother," authored by Jewel. This celebration was attended by an abundance of relatives and friends. Several years ago, Mother was posthumously recognized at an Eta Phi Beta event, which our sister Betty attended.

Mother first became a grandmother in 1963 and had 11 additional grandchildren by 1981, four of whom she obtained through Jewel's marriage and blended family. Mother was beloved by all of them and had established a unique relationship with each.

Aunt May and Mother often exchanged visits, as they were very loving sisters all of their lives. On holidays, Mother's Days, their birthdays or other celebrations, we siblings jointly honored them both. These events were held in several locales between Annapolis and Virginia Beach. We continued this practice until 1987, when our second mother, dear Aunt May, passed away.

Sometime in 1987, it was decided that Mother, all six of us, our spouses and some of our children would take a holiday excursion together to Freeport, The Bahamas. Jewel's husband, LeCount Davis, secured a group of rooms for us. Sixteen were in our party. The vacation time was spent swimming, fishing, shopping, eating, relaxing and luxuriating together. Our nephews, brother and sister Betty went charter boat fishing and caught a huge fish, a tuna, which the hotel chef prepared for our dinner meal. Mother had fun and was ecstatic to have us together having a jovial time. It was a trip we shall never forget.

Although retired, Mother continued her civic affiliations and volunteerism. She became a retired senior volunteer, taught crafts at a senior citizens center and gave her time at Richmond Community Hospital. She served on the 50th Reunion Committee of the Armstrong High School Class of 1929 and helped to implement fundraisers for its annual scholarship. In addition, several times each week, Mother visited Waller & Company for a few hours, where she served without compensation as a salesperson and greeter. She contributed to those in need by crocheting and donating more than 50 warm scarves to a homeless shelter.

Mother had a deep attachment to her Dungee kinfolk and on many occasions spoke about and visited her cousins. An early participant in Dungee Family Reunions, she encouraged us to attend as well. At a reunion held around the year 2000, some of us visited the Pamunkey and Mattaponi Indian Reservations in King William County. Mother would have been gratified because she had taken several of us to visit these reservations years earlier.

Mr. and Mrs. Thomas Carter and Mr. and Mrs. Russell Brown, her neighbors, were especially caring and accessible to Mother. Carolyn Brown, a native of South Carolina, who lived with Mother, became a compassionate friend. We appreciate their friendships with Mother.

We look back in amazement and wonder how Mother did it all. Mother lived a life of care and concern for us, other relatives, members of her church, the West End neighbors and the community at large. Mother was our ANGEL who helped us survive and thrive after the tragic and sudden loss of our daddy, while she herself was devastated. Mother was most remarkable, she accomplished so much and was such an enormous inspiration to those who knew and loved her. We were blessed to have her as OUR PHENOMENAL MOTHER. She departed our lives on March 27, 1993, at age 80.

Poems Mother Often Recited

Only One Mother – George Cooper

Hundreds of stars in the pretty sky,
Hundreds of shells on the shore together,
Hundreds of birds that go singing by,
Hundreds of lambs in the sunny weather.
Hundreds of dewdrops to greet the dawn,
Hundreds of bees in the purple clover,
Hundreds of butterflies on the lawn,
But Only One Mother the world wide over.

Somebody's Mother – Mary Dow Brine (1816–1913)

The woman was old and ragged and gray
And bent with the chill of the Winter's day.

The street was wet with a recent snow
And the woman's feet were aged and slow.

She stood at the crossing and waited long,
Alone, uncared for, amid the throng

Of human beings who passed her by
Nor heeded the glance of her anxious eyes.

Down the street, with laughter and shout,
Glad in the freedom of "school let out,"

Came the boys like a flock of sheep,
Hailing the snow piled white and deep.

Past the woman so old and gray
Hastened the children on their way.

Nor offered a helping hand to her
So meek, so timid, afraid to stir

Lest the carriage wheels or the horses' feet
Should crowd her down in the slippery street.

At last came one of the merry troop,
The gayest laddie of all the group;

He paused beside her and whispered low,
"I'll help you cross, if you wish to go."

Her aged hand on his strong young arm
She placed, and so, without hurt or harm,

He guided the trembling feet along,
Proud that his own were firm and strong.

Then back again to his friends he went,
His young heart happy and well content.

"She's somebody's mother, boys, you know,
For all she's aged and poor and slow,

"And I hope some fellow will lend a hand
To help my mother, you understand,

"If ever she's poor and old and gray,
When her own dear boy is far away."

And "somebody's mother" bowed low her head
In her home that night, and the prayer she said

Was "God be kind to the noble boy,
Who is somebody's son, and pride and joy!"

Memories of Our School Days

Richard and Jewel
in a Tom Thumb
wedding; he is wearing
a morning suit; her
dress is floor length!

Betty, 1956

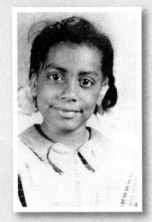

Lillian, 1956

Lillian, 1954

Richard, 1949

Jewel, 1949

Richard, 1948

Barbara and Betty in
third grade, 1954

**Richard dressed up
for an evening out**

**Claudette Carter, Richard, Jewel
and Karl Patterson, dressed
up for Charmerettes Ball**

**Betty and Barbara
on the way to
church, late 1950s**

**Barbara, 1962
Maggie Walker High
School, Homecoming
"Miss Walker"
First Runner-up**

**Clockwise from left: Joyce,
Barbara, Lillian, Betty,
Jewel and Richard, 1962**

Betty, 1962

Lillian, 1962

Joyce, 1962

**Betty and
Barbara, 1950s**

Mother Through the Years

At an NAACP celebration, Mother wears a crown.

Mother receives an award for her civic volunteerism, 1950s.

Mother and her dear friend, Mrs. Emily Baskerville, were community activists.

The President of The United States of America

Recognition to Mother from President Truman, December, 1948

AWARDS THIS CERTIFICATE OF APPRECIATION TO
Mrs. F. D. Waller
In grateful recognition of valuable service
contributed to the Nation as registrar
during the period of registration, August 30, 1948
Through September 18, 1948.

THE WHITE HOUSE

Mrs. F. D. Waller
West End Elementary School
Richmond 20
Virginia

A letter from First Lady Mamie Eisenhower, October 1955 to express appreciation for concern by West End Elementary School during President Eisenhower's illness.

The President and I are deeply grateful for your expression of good wishes and prayerful concern in his illness. I assure you your message has been helpful to him.

Mamie Doud Eisenhower

THE WHITE HOUSE
WASHINGTON

June 22, 1962

Dear Mrs. Waller:

Your kind message of birthday greetings pleased the President very much, and he has asked me to express his thanks. He is extremely grateful for your thoughtfulness.

Sincerely yours,

Evelyn Lincoln
Personal Secretary
to the President

Mrs. Florence D. Waller
2108 Rosewood Avenue
Richmond 20, Virginia

Note from President J. F. Kennedy's secretary, June 1962, thanking Mother for the birthday greeting she sent the president.

THE WHITE HOUSE

THE WHITE HOUSE
WASHINGTON

June 3, 1963

Dear Mrs. Waller:

Please accept the President's thanks for your kind birthday message. He sincerely appreciates your thoughtful greetings, and is especially grateful for your prayers.

Since you, too, observed your birthday on May 29, the President asked me to convey his cordial greetings and very best wishes.

Sincerely yours,

Evelyn Lincoln
Personal Secretary
to the President

Mrs. Florence D. Waller and Family
2108 Rosewood Avenue
Richmond 20, Virginia

THE WHITE HOUSE

Mrs. Florence D. Waller and Family
2108 Rosewood Avenue
Richmond 20, Virginia

Note from J. F. Kennedy to Mother, June 1963, to express thanks for his birthday message on their mutual birthday.

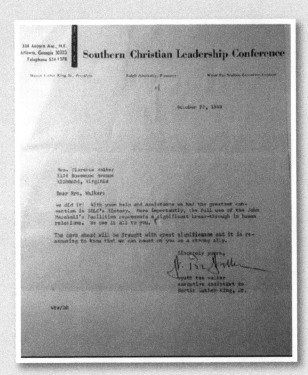

A letter from Wyatt Tee Walker in
appreciation for Mother's efforts
to help ensure full utilization of
John Marshall Hotel's facilities
for the Southern Christian
Leadership Conference,
October 22, 1963

A letter from Dr. Martin Luther King Jr.,
March 1964, declining an invitation to
speak at the Women's Club in spring, 1964

Mother As Teacher

> **Tribute to Mother from
> Beverly Brown,
> Kindergarten Class, 1956**

**Mother and her kindergarten class at
a school program in the late 1950s**

**Mother's kindergartners pose after
their academic presentation, 1950s**

**Mother's kindergartners pose at their
school's end-of-year presentation, 1950s**

Moore Street Church Willing Workers
Usher Board and Youth Ushers

Back row: Mother is 2nd from the right; Aunt Marie is 6th from the right; Aunt Geneva is seated at the center of the picture.

On far left, Mother; first row, 3rd from right, Aunt Geneva; second row, 4th from the left, Aunt Marie

First row, 2nd from left: Jewel,
Mother; 2nd row right: Richard

Clockwise: Aunt Marie, Velta
Carter, Letitia Peterson,
Mother and Helen Smith

Topettes Social Club

Mother hosts Topettes Social Club
Seated: Jessie Samuels, Margaret Jackson, Thelma Carter,
Aretha Franklin, Inez Quarles; Standing: Mother, Virginia
Mosby, Eliza Fountain and Emily Baskerville

Eta Phi Beta Sorority, Inc.

Mother with Eta Phi Beta Sorority, Alpha Delta Chapter
1st row, left to right: Mae Dunmore, our sister Lillian, unknown,
Letitia Peterson, Lillian Briggs and unknown.
2nd row: Mary McElwain, unknown, Virginia
Mosby, Odessa Thornton, Berbenia McDougald,
Rallene Hanson and Mother, early 1970s

Mother welcomes Eta Phi
Beta Sorors and Shads in
her capacity as Eastern
Regional Director.

Mother honored by Eta Phi Beta Sorority, 1973
Front row: Ta-Tanisha, Aubrey III, David and Rodney
2nd row: Uncle Buddy, Aunt May, Mother, Aunt Frances and Aunt Carrie
3rd row: Betty, Joyce, Barbara, Felandria, Michelle,
Lillian, Jean, Jewel, Rick and Rob

A Tribute to Our Mother

Mother, who is so sweet, so thoughtful, so kind
Always interested in her children, never leaving us behind
Mother, who told us to love, not to hate
To be on time for class, to never be late
Mother, who got us to church in rain and snow
Who was a beautiful wife and loved Daddy so
Mother, who taught us the best values in life
To get along with others, never creating strife
Mother, who 's so busy with her sorority and club news
But is never too busy to consider our views
Mother, who's known throughout the neighborhood
Collecting for charities – always doing good
We come here today in this fine November weather
To honor our Mother, who truly got it all together!

Richard, Jewel, Joyce, Lillian, Betty & Barbara
Read by Joyce, 11/18/73
Composed by Jewel

Dungee Family Reunions

An early Dungee Family Reunion. Mother is standing in the center and Aunt Carrie is seated on the right end.

Dungee Family Reunion. Front row, from left: kneeling, Uncle Buddy; 4th, Uncle Reggie, Cousin Roger Dungee. Back row, from left: 1st, Carolyn Dungee Contee; 4th, Doris Dungee Trotman; 5th, Mother; 8th, Aunt Carrie; from right: 4th, Aunt May; 5th, Aunt Frances

Joyous Occasions

We honored Mother with a party and a plaque on May 30, 1981. Seated: David and Aunt May. Standing, from left: Betty, Joyce, Richard, Mother, Jewel, Lillian and Barbara

Aubrey III plays a piano selection at the party.

June 9, 1981

To all my children namely – Richard & Jean, Jewel & LeCount, Joyce & Aubrey, Lill & George, Betty & Leonard, Barbara and Bobbie, and all the grandchildren.

Thanks a thousand times for one of the greatest days in my life. Surely the family and friends could say my children really love me not only in words but in action.

Everything was beautiful, the setting, the tributes, the presentation, food, friends and fellowship.

I will always remember May 30, 1981. Again many, many thanks and may God bless Each of you and keep you loving toward each other as you have shown your love to me.
Love,
Mother

Mother's Thank-You Note

You are invited to a Birthday Party in honor of Mrs. Florence Waller given by her children Saturday, May 30, 1981 from four until six o'clock Henderson Center Virginia Union University

Mother's Day 1987: Barbara, Mother, Lillian, Joyce, Jewel and Betty

Seated: Aunt May and Mother Standing, from left: Barbara, Betty, Jewel, Lillian and Joyce, early 1980s

Lillian, Betty, Jewel, Ta-Tianna,
Rev. Dr. Gilbert Campbell (pastor),
Leonetty, Barbara and Mother at
Moore Street Church, late 1980s

Mother is honored
on Mother's Day at
Jewel's home in 1987.

On Jewel's patio: Betty, Lillian, Barbara,
Mother, Joyce and Jewel, late 1980s

Mother, Joyce and Jean at
Moore Street Church, 1988

Richard, Joyce, Lillian, Mother, Betty,
Barbara and Jewel at the wedding of Michelle
Davis and Hansen Martin in 1985

Our 1987 Vacation in Freeport, The Bahamas

Mother and Jewel are relaxing in beautiful Freeport, The Bahamas.

Mother at the airport: she was happy and excited

LeCount and Mother

Rodney, David, Richard Jr. and Rob in Freeport

Fresh tuna for dinner, caught by Betty, Rodney, David and Rick

Betty, Richard and Jean

Joyce and Mother sharing time together in Freeport, The Bahamas

"O Christmas Tree,"
Mother at Jewel's
home, late 1980s

Mother on her
way to Waller
& Company's
90th Anniversary
celebration in 1990

Carla Waller, Jean,
Mother and Richard
"Alex" Waller IV

Mother, family and friends at Rodney's wedding
to Nataly; First row: Katie Cox, Lillian, Mother,
Ta-Tianna; Second row: Leonetty, Betty, Jewel;
Third row: Carolyn Brown, Jean, Barbara,
and Joyce; Back row: LeCount, Richard III,
Aubrey III, Aubrey Jr. and Haywood

What a special
day! Mother on
her 80th birthday.
This would be her
last, May 30, 1992.

Mother's last outing at the wedding
of Lillian's son, Rodney Thomas and
Nataly Garcia in 1991; Joyce, Barbara,
Mother, Lillian, Betty and Jewel

Tributes Read at
Mother's 80th Birthday Party/Luncheon
May 10, 1992

TO MY DARLING MOTHER – "CUTIE" –
FLORENCE LOUISE

A Beautiful Flower

Remembering – Calling "Richard Jr., Richard Jr., Richard Jr."

Betty and Barbara in your arms when you arrived home from the hospital,

Gently laying them on the dining room table.

Combing Lill's hair, using "mange."

Teaching Jewel and me to dust the baseboard and rounds on the chairs
On Cary Street.

Reading to us in the breakfast room.

Trips to Norfolk to see Joyce, riding on the Norfolk and Western Railroad.

Sunday School socks, ribbons, etc. on Saturday evenings.

Sunday evening after church at the Dairy Queen.

Corn pudding, macaroni and cheese, fried chicken breast, string beans and
Lemon meringue pie.

Willing Workers' meetings in the dining room.

Ms. Emily and Margaret's houses, where we had lots of fun.

Getting Mr. Norrell straight about my going to Canada with the "Gray Y" group
in 1949.

Encouraging me in school, as well as the many years after.

Always helping me in business.

Being a loving Grandmother to Ricky and David.

MOTHER, I LOVE YOU,

YOUR SON, RICHARD

MY MOTHER-IN-LAW

BY JEAN

From the very beginning
You took me in.
Made me a part of the family
A daughter, a friend.
Your warm smile,
Your loving ways,
Make you a mother-in-law
I like to praise.
With each passing day,
You become dearer to me
Than that first meeting
Which was thirty years ago and three.

MOTHER, I THANK YOU FOR

FROM JOYCE

Loving me and thinking of me, although I lived with Aunt May and
Uncle John. I always felt that I had 2 sets of parents.
Waiting until I arrived at Christmas to decorate the tree.
Christmases that were wonderful and magical.
Insisting to Jewel and Richard, "Where are you going that
you can't take Joyce?" I enjoyed going with them.
For having us participate in Bible School, Church, Sunday School,
Girl Scouts, Camp, and all other activities which helped
reinforce the Christian values you upheld.
For your commitment to community involvement, long before it was a
household phrase. All of us try to follow your example of caring
for others.
For looking so very beautiful when you and Daddy went out on social

occasions. Weren't you wearing Blue Waltz or Midnight Blue cologne?

For your encouragement, and insistence that we conduct ourselves like
"ladies and gentlemen."

Thank you for each and many more of these treasures of the heart.

May God continue to bless you and keep you in His Care.

Excerpts of Expressions from the Grandchildren

MY GRANDMOTHER

FROM DAVID

My Grandmother, whose caring hand and gentle heart fill my life with joy.

Whose dignity and perseverance give me inspiration to carry on.

Who is more endearing to me than the depths of the oceans, the world's grains of
sand.

Grandma, I love U, but these mere words and reflections could never show, how
I truly, truly, love you so.

REMINISCENCE OF TIME WITH MOMMY FLORENCE

BY AUBREY III

In the summer of 1979, I stayed at Mommy Florence's house for a week. That was
the first time I remember her telling me fascinating stories about her children in their grow-
ing-up years and how she and Grandfather Waller bought the house on Rosewood Avenue.
My most favorite memory of my time there was when Mommy Florence took me out to
dinner where she told me: that if I worked hard and tried my best, good things would come
to me. ***SHE WAS RIGHT!***

WHAT IS A GRANDMOTHER
FROM TA-TIANNA

Someone to wipe away the tears; someone who calms all our fears.
The reason we are here today…. Grandmother, we love you in every way.

REMINISCENCES
BY LEONETTY

The most remembered occasions: Mother's Day in 1984 when we visited a restaurant and Aunt Lill's house. On Mother's Day in 1991, we went to Aunt Joyce's home. On both occasions, we had lots of fun eating and playing Ping-Pong and other games. I also remember NiNi taking me downtown. We visited Uncle Richard's store, shopped and ate lunch. Then we visited a Senior Citizens Center and I helped pass out the lunches. I really liked helping out and enjoyed those times with NiNi.

HAPPY MOTHER'S DAY, MRS. WALLER
FROM CAROLYN BROWN, A DEAR FRIEND,
WHO SHARED MOTHER'S HOME

I would like to thank you for opening up your home to me as if I were one of your own children. Your love and hospitality have been wonderful. I hope God will always bless you and keep you in His care. Have a wonderful and blessed Mother's Day. I thank God our paths have crossed.

Part Five

Honoring Our Village

Our dearly beloved parents, grandparents, aunts and uncles on both the Waller and Dungee sides of the family were always loving, kind and thoughtful. They guided, inspired, encouraged and nurtured us. These adults were the village that made such a significant impact on our lives. All of Richard and Florence's children are eternally grateful for each one of them as well as their offspring, our three cousins. Most of these dear ancestors and cousins are now resting in peace in their heavenly homes, but we give them honor and reverence in this year of 2020. They were resilient and courageous and led by example. Their lives were grounded in their fervent Christian faith. We are proud of the shining legacy they left us.

Chapter 13

Our Cherished Parents

Richard Alexander Waller Sr.

Our loving and devoted father was born on November 8, 1908, in Richmond and was the son of Marcellus Carrington Waller and Nannie Brown Waller. Daddy completed Armstrong High School in 1927 and studied business subjects at Virginia Union University for two years. His lifelong work was with the family jewelry business, which his own dad had established in 1900.

Despite medical concerns, Daddy was always there for us; he was a loving, giving, affable father who cherished Mother and loved us. He was a family man; Mother, the six of us, the extended Waller-Dungee family and the business were Daddy's priorities. A dedicated husband, father, son and brother, he was a lifelong member of Moore Street Baptist Church. His life was directed by his Christian faith and this was reflected in his compassion and interactions with others.

At the age of 47, Daddy passed away suddenly in 1955 after attending the Armstrong-Maggie Walker football game. We mourn his loss and are forever grateful to God for every day we had with him. Daddy left us with so many treasured memories.

Florence Louise Dungee Waller

Our mother was born on May 30, 1912, in Richmond, daughter of Jesse Montague and Fannie Williams Dungee. Mother attended public schools and graduated in 1929 from Armstrong, the city's high school for Black students. Afterward, she enrolled at Virginia Union University and studied there for two years. Her college courses prepared her to teach kindergarten students and to operate a preschool. She trained many young minds, preparing her charges for public school and first grade. Mother was a caring and considerate wife and mother. She loved Daddy deeply and loved us deeply as well. She was smart, personable and possessed a keen intellect. Mother had a gregarious personality and judged all people by their character and behavior. She instilled this and many other important life lessons and principles in us.

During our formative years, Mother was always there for us as we all participated in a myriad of school, church and other events. She was our tower of strength and our phenomenal mother; we appreciated every moment with her. In addition to her parental responsibilities, Mother was immersed in the community, parents' groups at our schools, the church and in civic activities.

In 1955, after only 19 years of marriage, our daddy passed away suddenly and our lives changed forever. Mother nurtured and helped us adjust to life without our beloved daddy. We were blessed to spend many wonderful times with her as we honored her. In her mature years, we did our best to provide for her needs. In 1993, at age 80, our loving mother departed our lives. We thank God for allowing her 37 more years with us after losing our dad. We are reflections of Mother in our love, concern and respect for people.

Chapter 14

The Waller Village

Our Grandfather Marcellus Carrington Waller Sr., Grandmother Nannie Brown Waller and Grandmother Henrietta Winston Waller

Our grandfather, Marcellus Carrington Waller Sr., was born in Hewlett in Hanover County, Virginia, on April 10, 1873. He was the son of Mary Jane and Isaac Waller, who died when Grandpa was a young child; and he was reared by his grandparents. At age 14, Grandpa Waller came to Richmond with his Uncle Ben, who was a blacksmith. Grandpa also learned this trade before working as a delivery boy and porter at a grocery store. He later purchased and operated the grocery store, worked for an insurance company and invested in real estate prior to establishing his clock and watch repair business in 1900.

On March 21, 1895, Grandpa Waller married Nannie Brown Waller, a native of Cumberland County and the daughter of Joseph Brown and Bettie Booker Brown. Nannie passed away in 1917 after a lingering illness. Three years later, Grandpa married Henrietta Winston, a native of King William County.

An astute turn-of-the-century businessman and trailblazer, Grandpa started the firm M. C. Waller Jewelers in 1900. He later taught two of our uncles and our dad the skills necessary to fix clocks and watches. Until the 1940s, when Grandpa's health began to decline, the four of them successfully operated the store. The family members met the clock, watch and jewelry repair needs of customers throughout Richmond and the vicinity.

Our family continued to operate the store from its location at 1007 West Leigh for 51 years before closing in 1973. A component of the family jewelry enterprise continues today as Waller & Company Jewelers, and is owned by our brother, Richard Jr., and his sons. Grandpa Waller was a religious man who contributed to the business life of Colored Richmond, as well as to Richmond's religious and fraternal circles. Sadly, we did not know Grandmother Nannie because she died before we were born. Richard and Jewel were toddlers when Grandmother Henrietta passed away. Our beloved Grandpa died in 1957 at age 84.

James Clark Waller and Goldie Lee Waller

Uncle Clark, 1941

Uncle Clark and Aunt
Goldie, late 1940s or 1950s

Uncle Clark, Johnny
Dean holding Jewel,
and Grandpa, 1941

James Clark Waller, our Uncle Clark, was born December 2, 1895, and was married to the former Goldie Lee, born February 27, 1896. After the Selective Service Act was signed in May 1917, he registered for the draft. Uncle Clark's draft card indicated that he had a physical disability, and he worked as a chauffeur for Simon Sycle Company at 14 West Broad Street in Richmond. He was also a glass cutter for Sanders & Company at 1318 West Broad Street. Aunt Goldie was a laundress.

Through the years, Uncle Clark was a dapper dresser who carried a cane, wore a Panama straw boater hat and donned spectator shoes when he was going out to church and for special occasions.

When we were growing up, we were blessed to have Grandpa and Uncle Willie, Uncle Junius and Aunt Geneva, Uncle Clark and Aunt Goldie, and Uncle Tom and Aunt Marie living next door to each other. Their homes at 947, 949 and 1009 West Leigh Street, and M. C. Waller & Sons Jewelers, at 1007 West Leigh Street comprised the Waller compound. Uncle Clark died on October 7, 1959, at the age of 63; and Aunt Goldie died on September 24, 1966, at age 70.

William Waller

William Waller, our Uncle Willie, was born in 1901. We were told that as an adult, Uncle Willie was injured while in New York City. As a result, he seemed to have some challenges and was reclusive. He lived upstairs over the rear of the jewelry shop. From time to time, Richard, Jewel and other Waller relatives saw him briefly as he rushed out of the residence to visit a nearby grocery store and quickly returned. He disappeared in 1963; his date of death is unknown. No picture is available.

Marcellus Carrington Waller Jr., Geneva Spruill Waller and Elsie Aretha Waller

Uncle Junius, late 1950s

Marcellus Carrington Waller Jr., Uncle Junius, the second son of M. C. Waller and Nannie Waller, was born September 29, 1899. He preferred to be called Junius and legally changed his name. Throughout the years, Uncle Junius worked in the family watch and jewelry repair business. For several years, he operated a second jewelry store on First Street, not far from the Leigh Street shop. When he was called in 1941 to serve in World War II, this Waller & Sons store closed.

Uncle Junius was in the military from 1942 to 1945. Sometime during his tour in the military, he and his fellow soldiers were required to walk long distances carrying heavy loads. Uncle Junius was not accustomed to that level of physical exertion and he later reported to Richard Jr. that frequently his mates would carry him for part of the way.

After his military service, he joined his father and brothers at the Leigh Street store.

Aunt Geneva, 1960s

Uncle Junius married Geneva Spruill, who was born on March 9, 1911, in Edgecomb County, North Carolina. Her parents were Walter and Mary Williams Spruill.

A favorite pastime for Uncle Junius was hunting rabbits and small game in Hanover County. He delighted in fishing as well. In his later years, Richard Jr. drove Uncle Junius to Walter Reed Army Hospital in Washington, DC, for treatment related to his diabetes. Uncle Junius later developed blindness and had both legs amputated. He passed away on August 29, 1973.

Uncle Junius and Aunt Geneva were blessed with one daughter, Elsie Aretha, born April 16, 1945. Aunt Geneva was a longtime employee of the First Federal Savings and Loan Bank and the Virginia Federal Bank. She retired after more than 23 years of service. Aunt Geneva was an extraordinarily gifted seamstress; she created many beautiful and unique outfits for Elsie. She also made excellent pecan pies.

Aunt Geneva was an active, faithful and devoted member of Moore Street Church

Elsie, 1996

and served as a member of the church's Willing Workers Usher Board. In 1998, she received a certificate from the church for having been a member for 50 years. On June 15, 2002, Aunt Geneva died.

Our dear cousin Elsie attended Richmond Public Schools and received a bachelor's degree from Virginia State College (now University) in Petersburg. Elsie worked in the health care field and was employed by the Virginia Health Department as a laboratory technician for 22 years. Later, she worked for the Henrico County Public School System. Elsie is a member of Alpha Kappa Alpha Sorority, Inc., and was initiated in 1964 in Alpha Epsilon Chapter at Virginia State College. She is a lifelong member of Moore Street Church.

Marcellus Carrington Waller Jr. and Geneva Spruill Waller Family Pictures

**Uncle Junius and Aunt
Geneva, 1949**

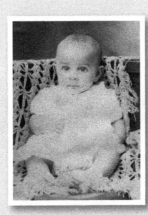

Elsie, 1945

Elsie, late 1940s

**Elsie, Aunt Geneva, Mother
and Rob, Lillian's son**

Lillian and Elsie, 1994

Bessie Aretha Waller Randolph and Henry Randolph

Aunt Aretha and Uncle Henry

Bessie Aretha Waller Randolph, Aunt Aretha, was born on October 27, 1902. She married Henry Randolph, who was the son of Mrs. Estelle Randolph, a Leigh Street neighbor. Mrs. Randolph taught piano at her home; Jean and Jewel were among her pupils. Aunt Aretha and Uncle Henry moved to Roxbury, Massachusetts, and lived there through the years. During this time, Aunt Aretha was a homemaker. Uncle Henry was a boxer, a prizefighter and a talented pianist. When he and Aunt Aretha visited our home when we were young, Uncle Henry always played the piano.

Uncle Henry and Uncle Tom, early years

Popular tunes, including "Honeysuckle Rose," were among his favorites.

Aunt Aretha passed away on November 1, 1956. Uncle Henry died on August 5, 1992.

Aunt Aretha in the 1930s or 1940s

Flemington R. Waller and Virginia Johnson Waller

Uncle Fleming

Flemington R. Waller, Uncle Fleming, was born November 14, 1907. Among Daddy's brothers, Uncle Fleming was the adventurous one. He attended Hampton Institute (now Hampton University) in Hampton, Virginia, and we are told that he was a student activist. Afterward, he worked and lived in Hawaii, Alaska, and later in Sacramento, California. He held positions with the federal government.

Whenever Uncle Fleming came home to visit, he brought photographic slides of many beautiful scenes of the faraway places where he lived and worked. Mother was responsible for many gatherings, sponsored by our elementary school's Parent-Teacher Association, where Uncle Fleming's pictures were presented. We looked forward to seeing these wonderful slides, which gave students, parents and teachers views of a world very different from our hometown. Whenever Uncle Fleming visited Richmond, the travel time was very extensive; as long as three days. All the family was happy to see their son, brother and uncle. Uncle Fleming was very fastidious and always well-dressed.

In 1941, at age 34, Uncle Fleming married Isabella Cox in Arizona. Fleming and Isabella were later divorced. Fleming was remarried on April 3, 1949, in Richmond to Virginia Johnson, a native of Goochland County, Virginia. The marriage was performed by the Reverend Dr. Gordon B. Hancock, pastor, Moore Street Church.

A memory we hold dear is Uncle Fleming's very lengthy blessing of the food (the grace) at the dinner following Dad's funeral and burial in November 1955. At that time, we had never heard a prayer that lasted so long and all six of us children became somewhat restless and agitated. We began giggling before the grace was finished. This had been a very difficult time for Mother and the children, but Uncle Fleming's grace served to bring some levity to a very dark and sad day. In 1966, Uncle Fleming passed away in Los Angeles, California, at age 58.

Flemington R. Waller and Virginia Johnson Waller Family Pictures

Famous boxer Joe Louis presents a certificate to Uncle Fleming.

Uncle Fleming speaks at a civic event.

Uncle Fleming and Daddy, 1948

Wedding of Uncle Fleming and Aunt Virginia on April 3, 1949.
Front row: Jean, Jewel, Richard and Elsie
From left: Uncle Tom, Aunt Marie, Grandpa, Uncle Fleming and Aunt Virginia, the Groom
and Bride, Daddy, Mother, Uncle Clark, Aunt Goldie, Uncle Junius and Aunt Geneva

Thomas Antonio Waller,
Marie Carter Waller and Jean Waller Brown

Aunt Marie, Uncle Tom and Cousin Jean

Thomas Antonio Waller, Uncle Tom, born June 29, 1911, was the youngest of Grandpa Waller's nine children. Uncle Tom attended Virginia Union University and worked in the family jewelry business alongside his father and brothers, Junius and Richard.

Thomas married the former Marie Carter, a native of Palmyra in Fluvanna County, Virginia (near Charlottesville). Aunt Marie's mother operated a general store near their home. Aunt Marie was one of three daughters and we fondly remember meeting her mother and her sisters Gladys (and daughter, Sandra) and Eleanor. Aunt Marie had come to Richmond to attend Virginia Union University, where she met Uncle Tom.

They were proud parents of one daughter, Jean Marie, who was born on February 3, 1938, just one week after Richard Jr. It was amazing that the brothers, who were very close, had their first offspring just one week apart. Growing up, Richard Jr. visited Uncle Tom and Aunt Marie often when they lived on Leigh Street. Richard Jr. helped himself to generous amounts of candy from the candy dish and enjoyed watching popular television shows of the day, including *Howdy Doody!* Aunt Marie and Uncle Tom lived in the Waller compound on Leigh Street for quite a few years before moving to Fendall Avenue in the Northside section of Richmond. Their beautiful new home had a large bedroom with a canopy bed and a backyard with a goldfish pond, and Jean had a dog named Buttons, whom we loved to play with.

Uncle Tom had a great sense of humor and had several witticisms. "Syllogistically speaking from a rambunctious standpoint, the oxidation of the verb is quite absurd" and "It is so simple a baby can understand it, but so profound, philosophers ponder its profundity," were two of his phrases that usually elicited hearty laughter.

Both Uncle Tom and Aunt Marie were members of Moore Street Baptist Church. He was a lifelong member and served as a deacon for many years. Aunt Marie was an active member of the Willing Workers Usher Board and served as a deaconess. She was an excellent homemaker and a fashionable dresser.

They were married about 1937 and were together for 60 years. They both departed this life in 1997. Services were held for Aunt Marie on May 8, 1997. Uncle Tom passed away shortly thereafter and his services were held on July 14, 1997. Services and interment for both were at Forest Lawn Cemetery.

Their dear daughter, Jean Marie, received her elementary and secondary education in the Richmond Public Schools and graduated from Armstrong High School. She had a beautiful childhood growing up with many of her cousins and friends in Richmond and in Palmyra. She joined Moore Street Church, where her parents and many relatives had long-standing ties.

During her youth, Jean studied piano and trained for several years with a local dance group. She was one of the group's premier dancers and repeatedly had solo performances and lead roles during the troupe's annual recitals. She was an active member of Richmond's Gay Misses Club, which held beautiful holiday celebrations each year.

In 1959, Jean graduated from Hampton Institute with a bachelor's degree in biology and chemistry, and later she received a master's degree in guidance, from Columbia University in New York City. At Hampton, Jean was an honor student. She joined Alpha Kappa Alpha Sorority, Inc., and was active in it and other student organizations.

Jean spent her professional career as a dedicated teacher and administrator in the Richmond Public School System. She taught chemistry and biology, was a guidance counselor and ended her career as the director of Human Resources. She took an early retirement in 1995 to come home and take care of her ailing parents.

On November 17, 1984, Jean married LeRoy Brown, a native of King William County and a graduate of Norfolk State. As a couple, they enjoyed life to its fullest. Jean was a very social person with an outgoing personality and was loved by all. She liked to dance and entertain. Jean and LeRoy traveled extensively, taking more than 20 cruises in and outside of the U.S. Several trips were with cousins Richard, Jewel and Joyce and their spouses, and Betty. Jean was a member of AKA Sorority, Upsilon Omega Chapter and its chorale; the Richmond Chapter of the National Epicureans, Inc.; and the Bon Tons Social Club. LeRoy is an active member of Kappa Alpha Psi Fraternity, the Thebans Club and the Guardsmen.

Jean always was fond of pets, especially her little miniature poodles. In recent years, she doted on Sidney and then Fritz.

In her last few years, Jean began to have health problems. Despite these issues, she remained vibrant and active and continued her travels with LeRoy and the Guardsmen, and participated in her line dancing classes. On May 17, 2017, at age 79, our cousin Jean departed this life. A service of her heavenly flight was held at Moore Street Church on May 27 with interment near her parents at Forest Lawn Cemetery.

Thomas Antonio Waller and
Marie Waller Family Pictures

Uncle Tom and Aunt
Marie about the time of
their wedding in 1937

Jean, Uncle Tom
and Aunt Marie

Jean in ballet
costume,
early 1950s

Jean, late 1950s

Jean and LeRoy

Jean—how lovely!

Jean and LeRoy
A special time together

Jean and her dog Fritz

Chapter 15

The Dungee Village

Our Grandfather Jesse Montague Dungee Sr. and Grandmother Fannie Williams Dungee

Grandpa Jesse Dungee

**Grandmother
Fannie Dungee**

Grandpa Dungee, Jesse Montague Dungee, born in 1878, was the son of John Beverly and Ethelin Dungee. His parents were distant cousins, part Native American, had ties to the Mattaponi and Pamunkey tribes of the Powhatan Confederacy and were natives of King William County, Virginia. We are told that no Dungees were ever born into slavery.

Grandpa Dungee lived in New York for a time before returning to Virginia, where he met our grandmother, Fannie Aribelle Williams. Grandmother Fannie was born November 16, 1878, in Anacostia, DC. Her mother, Mary L. Robinson Williams, was born into slavery in Caroline County about 1852.

Our Dungee grandparents married on June 25, 1902, in Manhattan, New York, and they returned to live in Virginia. Grandmother Fannie was a cultured, refined and educated lady, who had completed training at the Richmond Colored Normal School in 1900. Her first teaching assignment was with the King William County Schools in West Point where she met Grandpa. Having married, Grandmother Fannie was no longer able to teach in the state of Virginia.

During the years, Grandpa was employed by Old Dominion Iron and Steel, while Grandmother Fannie was a laundress, operated a kindergarten from her home and reared foster children.

Grandmother Fannie passed away in 1943 when only three of us had been born; we barely remember her. Grandpa Dungee remarried after the passing of Grandma Fannie and later moved to Norfolk before he died in 1962 at age 83.

Jesse Montague Dungee Jr. and Carrie Chambers Dungee

Uncle Buddy

Jesse M. Dungee Jr., our uncle Buddy and Mother's only brother, was born March 5, 1903. He was married to Carrie Chambers Dungee, a native of Fine Creek, West Virginia. She was the daughter of John L. and Lelia Lewis Chambers and was born May 19, 1907. Uncle Buddy's marriage to Aunt Carrie was his third; his previous marriages ended in divorce before we knew those aunts. We loved Aunt Carrie and felt close to her.

Her family moved to St. Albans, West Virginia, and Aunt Carrie later moved to Richmond. There, she was educated at Van de Vyver School and the St. Philip School of Nursing, where she became a licensed practical nurse. Aunt Carrie was a private duty nurse for quite some time; she was loved by her patients, who showered her with gifts and accolades.

Uncle Buddy and Aunt Carrie lived on Randolph Street, a few blocks from our West Cary Street home. In later years, they moved to Powhatan Street and remained in the West End. Aunt Carrie and Uncle Buddy both were good cooks who loved to cook and to eat. Whenever we visited, they had large platters of good food on the table; chicken, fish, pork chops and more, and enough for a dozen people, even though all this food was for just the two of them.

Every year on our birthday, Aunt Carrie and Uncle Buddy treated each of us with a delicious birthday cake from Thalhimer's Department Store Bakery. When our birthday

Aunt Carrie

was near, we gleefully anticipated this special extravagance from them.

Uncle Buddy worked at Old Dominion Iron and Steel Works on Belle Isle. He later worked at Broad Street Railroad Station, where he was a porter who transported the remains of soldiers killed in World War II, and also newspapers that were conveyed from New York.

We often visited Aunt Carrie and Uncle Buddy on Sunday afternoons. They were especially fond of Lill, and she spent many nights with them. Lill liked taking walks with the couple to the nearby cemetery and the railroad tracks close to their home. She occasionally accompanied them when they visited West Virginia. Uncle Buddy was a great teaser and used special humorous terms of endearment for all of us. Uncle Buddy and Aunt Carrie were caring, generous relatives, whose home was always open to family. They cared for Aunt Carrie's sister, Mary Frances Chambers; her Uncle Prince and her nephews, who visited each summer from West Virginia. Aunt Carrie and Uncle Buddy were a devoted couple, who loved and embraced the next generation of great-nieces and -nephews, our children. Aunt Carrie departed this life on March 7, 1982, followed by Uncle Buddy on January 25, 1984.

Jesse Montague Dungee Jr. and Carrie Chambers Dungee Family Pictures

Aunt Carrie

Uncle Buddy, Aunt Carrie, Uncle Reggie, Aunt Frances, Grandpa and Mother

Uncle Buddy at retirement, 1969

Uncle Buddy, kneeling on left with friends, 1940s

Lillian May Dungee Henderson and
Dr. John Bennett Henderson

Aunt May

Uncle John

Lillian May Dungee Henderson, Aunt May, was born on July 16, 1904. Aunt May was named for her aunt, Lillian Edith Williams Jones. She was "big sister" to Mother, Florence, and Aunt Frances; she was always supportive of her younger sisters. The bond between the three of them was unbreakable. Although Aunt Frances lived in New Jersey, Aunt May visited her annually. Due to their proximity to each other, Mother and Aunt May were like "two fingers on the same hand." Aunt May visited Mother often and, in the summer, stayed for periods of time so that Mother could attend conventions and other civic gatherings.

Aunt May completed Armstrong High School in 1922 and Armstrong Normal School in 1926. Normal schools were institutions that prepared high school graduates to teach. She began her teaching career in the Richmond Public School System; she taught at Elba Elementary initially. She received her bachelor's degree in education from Hampton Institute in 1939 and later earned a master's degree at Columbia University in New York City in 1949.

During this period, Blacks could not enroll in courses at White colleges and universities in Virginia. The state of Virginia funded superior postgraduate studies for numerous Black educators in out-of-state universities. Other southern states enacted the same restrictions.

Many Colored teachers obtained advanced degrees at colleges and universities that were much more prestigious than those located in Virginia. Aunt May, like hundreds of other Colored educators, decided to leave the state for postgraduate study. She traveled to New York over a span of several summers and completed her requirements for a master's degree in education.

Aunt May and Uncle John met in Richmond while Uncle John was an undergraduate student at Virginia Union University (VUU) and Aunt May was a teacher at Randolph Elementary School. At that time, she resided with Great-aunt Lillie at 723 West Marshall Street. Great Aunt Lillie was an entrepreneur who had operated her own beauty parlor from her home, which she purchased prior to 1922. Aunt May and Uncle John quietly married on September 3, 1930, in Frederick, Maryland, as Virginia policies did not allow married teachers to continue teaching in public schools. Their marriage was not recorded in Virginia!

She taught and cared for Grandmother Fannie, who had an extended illness, until Grandmother passed away in 1943. Following this sad event, Aunt May and Uncle John moved to Norfolk, where he began as pastor of Bank Street Baptist Church and she restarted her career with Norfolk Public Schools. She was Uncle John's most ardent supporter. Theirs was a very happy marriage.

Aunt May taught in Norfolk until 1970, when she retired after 42 years as a teacher in Virginia. She was a master teacher who cared deeply about her pupils. At the same time, she had high standards and expectations for all of her nieces and nephews, her students and her coworkers. She was our "no-nonsense" aunt. We could read her facial expressions; we knew if she was pleased or displeased with our behavior; we wanted her to be pleased. Few of us ever wanted to disappoint her. She was caring. For example, when the circus came to town, she transported 25 or 30 of her school charges, a carload at a time, to the arena, where they waited safely until all were there. She prepared Christmas and Thanksgiving parties for her students during the school day, supplying holiday dinners with all the trimmings. For many children whose families were impoverished, these celebrations were very meaningful.

Uncle John was born May 6, 1908, in Newport News, Virginia, to the Reverend Hamilton Henderson and Mrs. Mamie Hamlett Henderson. Our connection with Uncle John's family gave us another set of grandparents, aunts, uncles and cousins. His siblings were Dr. Thomas H. Henderson (Kate, daughter Tommyzee); Welton H. Henderson (Mary Lou); Pearl H. Wood (C. Barford, daughter Pamela); and Dr. Mary H. Wright (Dr. Jeremiah Sr., daughter LaVerne and son Jeremiah Jr.). The ties between the Henderson family and the Waller-Dungee family commenced in 1930 and continue today.

Uncle John's religious training began at home. He earned a bachelor of arts from VUU in 1930; a bachelor of divinity from Oberlin College in 1932 and a master of science from Hampton Institute in 1940. Throughout his pastorates, he pursued additional study at seminaries in Richmond, New York City, Chicago and Washington, DC. In recognition of his very diligent commitment to the church and community, VUU conferred upon him an honorary doctor of divinity (DD) degree in 1952.

He first pastored at Trinity Baptist Church in Newport News; he also taught for Newport News Public Schools, but was fired due to his efforts to obtain equal pay for Black educators. Uncle John was pastor of Bank Street Baptist Church for 31 years, from 1943 until his untimely death on July 14, 1974. Uncle John was passionate about Bank Street Church's involvement in the movement for social justice. In the late 1960s, he went with a group of local clergy to Chicago for about 10 days, where he interacted with the poor and survived on $5.00/day for meals (housing was provided), to gain a greater awareness of the needs of persons living in poverty. Uncle John had an earnest interest in the youths of the community; Bank Street Church implemented a program at the church whereby neighborhood youth could come after school for recreation, mentoring and help with homework.

Uncle John deeply loved the Bank Street Church family. Under his dynamic leadership, the church, after much study and prayer, decided to relocate from its downtown site at Bank and Charlotte Streets to 7036 Chesapeake Boulevard in Norfolk. The move was made because the downtown area was being redeveloped into business, shopping and tourist attractions; most church members no longer lived close by.

While at Bank Street, Uncle John became the first president of the American Baptist Churches of the South in 1970. He served as president of both the Baptist General Association of Virginia and the Lott Carey Baptist Foreign Mission Convention; and he was a member of the executive board, Virginia Conference of NAACP Branches. He was also a member of Alpha Phi Alpha Fraternity and the Masons and was affiliated with many other civic and religious organizations. For a number of years, he taught extension classes for Virginia Union's School of Religion, and he was an associate professor at Norfolk State University.

Aunt May and Uncle John always assisted people who needed their help, giving no thought to one's social station, living conditions or educational level. They did this without fanfare and as if it were the most natural thing in the world. Aunt May was the beloved

"First Lady" of Bank Street Church, yet she was a woman fully able to stand on her own. She was involved in many church-related organizations and several Ministers' Wives associations. In addition, she was a member of Cloverleaf, a social club that offered fellowship and fun.

Aunt May and Uncle John supplied a second very loving home for Joyce. Mother, Daddy and all of Joyce's siblings were frequent visitors too, up until Daddy's demise. Jewel and Richard often rode the train to Norfolk to visit. On occasion Lillian, Betty and Barbara, as had Jewel and Richard, visited and participated in Vacation Bible School, Sunday School and other church events.

A fantastic cook, Aunt May was very organized, always planned ahead and was well prepared in the event unexpected guests came to dinner or to spend the night at the parsonage. Pies, cakes, crab cakes, Smithfield ham, hot rolls and choice breakfast weekend foods were her specialties. Aunt May welcomed many of Joyce's friends to their family's Sunday dinners, where Aunt May set an elegant table and prepared a wonderful feast. Joyce's guests helped to clear the table and with washing and drying the many dirty dishes; what a small price to pay for a mouthwatering repast and the stimulating conversation that ensued. There were few, if any, refusals of an invitation to dine with the family.

When Joyce's son Aubrey III was born in 1967, Aunt May and Uncle John, along with Mother, Aubrey Sr. and Sophronia Baden, became proud grandparents. Uncle John and Aunt May purchased a Junior Life NAACP membership for Aubrey III before he was two years old; it was presented to him in Norfolk at the NAACP fall banquet in 1969.

Aunt May and Uncle John were Joyce's foster mother and father from the age of three, and a second set of parents to the rest of Florence and Richard's children. Joyce went to Norfolk and lived with them until she enrolled at Howard University and later married Aubrey.

Lillian also lived with Aunt May and Uncle John while she attended Booker T. Washington High School beginning as a high school junior. She graduated in 1962. Both Betty and Barbara resided with Aunt May and Uncle John for four years while they earned their undergraduate degrees at Norfolk State. Joyce stated, "When we lived with them during our years as high schoolers and collegians (not the easiest of years to live with teens), Aunt May and Uncle John loved us and treated each one of us as a precious daughter. They made certain that we did not lack for adequate spending money or any essentials."

No graduation, birthday or other achievement occurred without Aunt May and Uncle John's loving acknowledgment and often their presence. Upon Uncle John's death on July 13, 1974, Aunt May continued to work in many aspects of Bank Street Church, until her health declined. She spent time with Joyce and Aubrey in Annapolis, but could not be persuaded to make a permanent move to live with them. She had many active and productive years before passing away on February 5, 1987. She and Uncle John are much loved and sorely missed.

Lillian May Dungee Henderson and Dr. John Bennett Henderson Family Pictures

**Aunt May
A beautiful pose**

**Aunt May as a
teenager, about 1920**

Aunt May, 1930s

**Uncle John receives
doctor of divinity
(VUU), 1952**

**Uncle John and Aunt May
are feted by Bank Street
Church to celebrate their
25th wedding anniversary,
September 3, 1955.**

**Bank Street
sanctuary, 1940s**

Aunt May, Uncle John
and Joyce, early 1960s

Aunt Frances, Aunt May
and Mother in 1970 at
Aunt May's Retirement.
She taught for 43 years.

Wedding of Mary E. Wright, Uncle John's sister, and the Reverend Jeremiah
A. Wright Sr. on June 8, 1938. Left to right: our dad, Richard Waller Sr.;
the father of the bride, the Reverend Hamilton Henderson; our Uncle
John, the Reverend John Henderson; our cousin John Dean, ringbearer;
to the groom's right: brother of the bride, Welton Henderson; and third
to the left of the bride, Mrs. Jocelyn Pretlow Goss, bridesmaid

Aunt May

They call her Lill, but to us she's Aunt May,
When we were little, it was at her house we'd stay;
She guided us, advised us with a real firm hand;
Aunt May was a lady who always took a stand;

There were playgrounds and movies near Bank and Charlotte Street
When we visited Aunt May, plenty of good food did we eat!
We played, went to Bible School and Bank Street on Sunday;
And caught the train to Richmond the first thing on Monday;

Aunt May and Uncle John had Richard and Jewel come for the day;
But Joyce was Mother's child who came to stay;
They reared her, taught her and sent her to school;
She had nice manners, and always observed the golden rule;
Later Lill, Betty and Barbara came for their education;
And lived with Aunt May until time for graduation;

Whether Baptism, awards day or high school prom;
Aunt May was always with us, she was our second mom;
There is no kinder, sweeter Aunt in this world today;
Than Mother's oldest sister, our AUNT MAY.

Composed by Jewel, 1979

The Reverend Hamilton Martin Henderson and Mrs. Mamie Hamlett Henderson

The Waller-Dungee family connected to the Henderson family in 1930, with the marriage of Lillian M. Dungee and John B. Henderson. The Reverend Hamilton Martin Henderson (1873–1965) was a native of Vance County, North Carolina. He was one of 13 children born to James and Tabiatha Henderson. He moved to Mecklenberg County, Virginia, while he was a teenager. In 1902, he graduated from the Theological Department of Virginia Union University. For more than 50 years, Reverend Henderson pastored various Baptist churches in Virginia. In addition, he provided leadership in both private and parochial schools. During his last 25 years as an educator, he taught in Prince George and Surry counties in Virginia. His interests in youth and concern for their education inspired a large number of them to attend college.

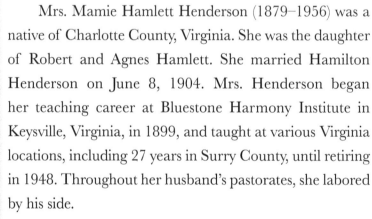

Mrs. Mamie Hamlett Henderson (1879–1956) was a native of Charlotte County, Virginia. She was the daughter of Robert and Agnes Hamlett. She married Hamilton Henderson on June 8, 1904. Mrs. Henderson began her teaching career at Bluestone Harmony Institute in Keysville, Virginia, in 1899, and taught at various Virginia locations, including 27 years in Surry County, until retiring in 1948. Throughout her husband's pastorates, she labored by his side.

The couple had eight children, three of whom perished at an early age. Their five remaining offspring were very accomplished and reflected their parents' dedication to Christian education and ministry, social justice, community service and musical pursuits.

Photos of Offspring of
The Reverend and Mrs. Hamilton
Martin Henderson

The Rev. Dr. John B. Henderson (1908–1974) and Mrs. Lillian May Dungee Henderson (1905–1987) were our dear uncle and aunt and Joyce's beloved foster parents. Their wedding date: September 3, 1930

Dr. Mary Henderson Wright (1916–2005), teacher, high school principal, religious speaker; and the Rev. Dr. Jeremiah A. Wright Sr. (1909–2000), pastor of Grace Baptist Church, Philadelphia, humanitarian and spiritual leader

Mr. Welton H. Henderson (1912–1976), elementary school principal, Norfolk; and Mrs. Mary Lou Tyler Henderson (1911–2001), professor at Norfolk State College

Dr. Thomas H. Henderson (1910–1970), educator and president of Virginia Union University, Richmond; daughter Tommyzee; and Mrs. Kate Gilpin Henderson (1900–1976), school counselor, mentor and advisor, Richmond

Pamela Wood (1943–2018), and her parents: Mrs. Pearl Henderson Wood (1914–1998), teacher, musician and composer; and Clinton Barford Wood (1913–1971), social worker, Richmond

Children of Drs. Jeremiah A. and Mary H. Wright

Dr. William R. Miner, pioneer of innovative programs in urban development with the US Agency for International Development; and Mrs. LaVerne Wright Miner, retired after employment as a world language teacher in Watertown, Massachusetts; mentor and musician. LaVerne and Bill have a son, Edward Wright, and daughter-in-law, Meghan.

Dr. Jeremiah A. Wright Jr., Pastor Emeritus, Trinity United Church of Christ, Chicago, Illinois; and Dr. Ramah E. Wright, associate pastor, Covenant United Church of Christ in South Holland, Illinois. They are parents of Janet Marie Moore, Jeri Lynne Wright, Jamila Nandi Wright, Nikol Reed and Nathan Reed; and grandparents of Jeremiah Antonio Wright Haynes, Jazmin Lynne Hall, Steven Lawrence Moore and twins Adia Naja and Adani Nadira Wright.

Daughter of Dr. Thomas and Mrs. Kate G. Henderson

Ms. Tommyzee Henderson Suggs, retired after employment as a social worker with Howard University, Washington, DC. She is mother of Kasan Brigman and Kashmir Spells and is grandmother of Kalaurie Taylor, Chirone and Khloe Brigman.

Daughter of Mrs. Pearl H. and Mr. C. Barford Wood

Ms. Pamela Wood, an acclaimed vocalist and operatic singer, was a music educator at MIT after her career as a recitalist. She is mother of Ayanna Moore and Amara Vaughn (Daron) and grandmother of Derek Moore and Scott Evelyn Vaughn.

Frances Queen Dungee Dean Jerome,
Reginald Brown Jerome and John Beverly Dean

Aunt Frances

Uncle Reggie

Frances Queen Dungee Dean Jerome, Aunt Frances, the second daughter of Jesse and Fannie, was born December 9, 1910. She apparently was a very high-spirited and fun-loving child. As the story goes, she once danced on a table at home and FELL OFF! She married Robert E. Dean while in her early twenties and had one son, John Beverly Dean, Johnny, who was the apple of her eye. After Aunt Frances and Robert Dean divorced, Aunt Frances moved to New Jersey. While we are not certain where she completed her licensed practical nurse training, she was never without employment as a hospital nurse or as a private duty nurse. Her patients thought highly of her and often gave her lovely gifts of all kinds.

In 1944, Aunt Frances married Reginald Brown Jerome, who was born in 1902 to Arthur Jerome and Florence Dungee (the same name as our mother!) Jerome. Uncle Reggie worked in New York. At one time, he was a waiter on a boat that traveled from New York City to Connecticut. He later worked on the railroad. Uncle Reggie was always kind to us and he most especially loved his "Babe," Aunt Frances, as he affectionately named her.

They lived in Jersey City, then purchased a home in Plainfield, New Jersey, in the mid-fifties. Their home was near several Dungee cousins, including Fred Dungee, his wife Marian and their children, Marcia and Fred Jr.; and cousin Catherine Dungee. The Dungees and the Jeromes frequently gathered at Aunt Frances' home to play pinochle, their favorite card game, with great intensity. Aunt Frances and Uncle Reggie occasionally enjoyed going to jazz nightclubs in New York. Aunt Frances and Uncle Reggie once took Aunt May and Joyce to the supper club Red Rooster, where Congressman Adam Clayton Powell's wife, Hazel Scott, had performed years earlier.

Aunt Frances was a fabulous cook and an immaculate homemaker. Almost as soon as breakfast was completed, she began planning for dinner; the table was set and other preparations were made for yet another delicious homemade repast. It was through Aunt Frances that we Waller nieces learned to enjoy peach and blueberry cobbler and New York cheesecake. Whenever she visited our home, she brought a suitcase laden with goodies that included a variety of peanuts, candies and cookies.

On one occasion, Lillian, Betty and Barbara visited Aunt Frances and Uncle Reggie in Jersey City. They traveled by train and they have lasting memories of enjoying a boat tour of Manhattan and seeing the Statue of Liberty. During an extremely heavy rainfall, after the couple had moved to Plainfield, runoff from the nearby Watchung mountains flooded Aunt Frances' basement up to its ceiling. She and Uncle Reggie suffered quite a financial loss. That did not deter them; they made the necessary repairs to their basement and also added two rooms to their home, which became a cozy and inviting "guest suite."

Aunt Frances and Uncle Reggie were active members of their church in Plainfield. In 1972, when Aunt May and Uncle John moved from their 1301 Merrimac Avenue residence in Norfolk to their new home in Virginia Beach, Aunt Frances and Uncle Reggie relocated to Virginia and lived with them. After Uncle John's death in 1974, Aunt Frances and Uncle Reggie found an apartment in Norfolk and seemed happy there for a number of years before both of them suffered ill health. Uncle Reggie passed away suddenly in 1986. Aunt Frances, who had some dementia, relocated to Hampton, Virginia. Later, her son Johnny took her to live with him in Nashville, where she passed away in 1989.

Cousin Johnny

Aunt Frances' son Johnny, the first Dungee grandchild of our generation, was born in Richmond on September 9, 1930. Cousin Johnny attended boardingschool in Bordentown, New Jersey, for several years. He had the "gift of gab," and managed, many times, to find lucrative and significant employment in marketing jobs. He was always well groomed and well spoken; he was a natural salesman. Johnny also was an accomplished journeyman printer and sometimes worked in Washington, DC, Virginia, and Maryland, plying his trade with various printing companies.

He was the father of several children and was married a number of times. We were acquainted with just one of his children, his son Reginald Dean, whose mother was Liz. By 1994, Johnny was a double amputee, due to diabetes. Most of us last saw him that year at our sister Lillian's home for her 50th birthday celebration. Our niece Ta-Tanisha Nealy Walton, Barbara's daughter, recalls Johnny's kindness to her while she was a student at Norfolk State in the 1990s.

> Johnny Dean was very kind to me and a great support during my time as a college student. It was nice to know that a family member was in the area that I could contact. My stay (with him) was only for a very short time, perhaps a few days/weeks if I can recall. I remember being impressed with his ability to drive even though he had prostheses; and he always had a lady friend nearby. I rode in the back seat while he and his friend talked and laughed. He often took me to (dinner at) Piccadilly in Military Circle Mall or Feather and Fin on Tidewater Drive on several Sunday afternoons. When I received word that Grandmother Florence was gravely ill, he picked me up and drove me to Richmond. In addition, he made arrangements to transport me to Tidewater Park Elementary School, which was my first teaching assignment, for a few weeks and was with me when I bought my first car back in 1994.

Johnny Dean passed away January 21, 1999, in Okmulgee, Oklahoma.

Frances Queen Dungee Dean Jerome and Reginald Jerome Family Pictures

Aunt Frances

Johnny as a toddler

Aunt Frances, Johnny and Uncle Reggie

Aunt Frances and Uncle Reggie's wedding celebration

Aunt Frances and Mother

Mother, Lillian and Johnny at Aunt Frances' burial

Part Six

Sharing Our Stories

As we examined our adult lives, it was evident that each of us lived a life of integrity and good character, and we each had a desire to achieve. These values were bequeathed to us by our village and sustained by our aspirations and Christian faith. The injustices we experienced on an ongoing basis raised our consciousness of the systems in place that created and maintained racial inequality in every aspect of our lives. Despite these challenges, we were not deterred.

We had different career paths and interests, and worked ardently in the vocations we selected. Honors and recognition were extended to us for our various talents, skills and contributions. We are confident that successive family generations will do their best to follow and surpass the example set by their ancestors.

We six siblings have always had loving relationships and have been close since childhood. We are best friends and have provided love and support through life's difficult and joyous times. Richard, our big brother, and Jewel, our oldest sister, were protective of the younger sisters. Joyce, though living out of town, was an integral part of our Waller tribe. Lillian, Betty and Barbara, our more youthful trio, were especially loved and nurtured by the older three.

Through the years, these relationships deepened and matured. We value our love for each other. We hope that the next generation will continue to express their affection for, and devotion to, one another. The love, trust, and fondness that we have experienced mirror that of our beloved parents and other family members.

Chapter 16

Profiles in Excellence and Memorable Times Together

Richard Alexander Waller Jr.

Richard A. Waller Jr.

Richard, first child and only son of Richard and Florence Waller, was born on January 27, 1938. Richard graduated from Maggie Walker High School in 1956 and began working full time in the family jewelry firm. He enrolled in college-level courses at Richmond's Virginia Polytechnic Institute, and completed further study for jewelry and watch repairing and diamond setting.

Richard met Jean Jones in 1957 through a mutual friend and they married on December 26, 1959, at the Waller family home on Rosewood Avenue. The Reverend Dr. Gordon B. Hancock, pastor of Moore Street Baptist Church, performed the marriage ceremony. Four months before they married, Richard purchased a beautiful home in the Maymont section of the West End; Jean and Richard remained there until they purchased their second home in the city's Southside in 1993.

Richard, owner of Waller & Company Jewelers, followed his father and uncles into the business and has worked in jewelry service and sales for his entire life. Always diligent, and often working two jobs in his early years, Richard states, "I was not born with a silver spoon, but with a wooden spoon and that spoon had a hole in it." In 1968, Richard established his own jewelry store in downtown Richmond. Five years later, the family firm,

M. C. Waller & Sons, located on West Leigh Street, was closed. Richard then combined his firm and the Leigh Street shop into a single enterprise. His beautiful store was one of the first Black-owned companies to be located on Broad Street, at the time, a major shopping area. All the family was filled with pride at this major accomplishment.

Richard and Jean were blessed with two sons—Richard Alexander III and David Marcellus. Both sons matriculated in the Richmond Public Schools and pursued higher education. Richard and Jean have one grandson, Richard IV, "Alex," who is the son of Richard III and Carla Cousins Waller. In 2013, Richard III married Dr. Kim Lacy Waller, who is a loving daughter-in-law and a great asset to the family jewelry business.

Jean Jones Waller

Jean Frances Jones Waller

Jean was born on February 18, 1939, in a rural area in Scotland Neck, North Carolina. She lived on her parents' farm and was the youngest of six children of Eliza Tootle Jones and James Jones. Her siblings were Morris, Hilda, Alfreda, Ethel and James Douglas. Jean attended Norfleet Elementary School through eighth grade and then Brawley High School for grades nine through twelve, graduating in 1956. She was baptized at age 12 and joined the Kehukie Baptist Church in Scotland Neck. The Reverend C. C. Clark was pastor.

The highlight of Jean's elementary school days was Picnic Day, similar to May Day, when parents packed food and brought it to school. Students wore costumes and each class performed a little skit or dance. Following a scrumptious lunch, a softball game was organized in the afternoon and a play performed by students was held at night. High school days were also exciting. For Jean, basketball and making the team in her first year, and attending the Junior-Senior Prom were two of her most memorable high school events. The junior class was always responsible for the expenses of the prom, leaving the seniors free for all other expenses associated with graduating.

In 1957, Jean moved to Richmond and enrolled in Smith-Madden Business School, graduating in 1959. Jean and Richard were married after she completed studies at Smith-Madden.

Jean worked as secretary to a home demonstration agent and at Bellwood, the U.S. Defense General Supply Center, where she was employed as a typist and concluded her time there as a buyer. After a few years' hiatus following son David's birth, Jean filled the position of secretary for Richmond Public Schools, serving at Armstrong High, John F. Kennedy High and Mary Mumford Elementary, where she retired in 2003, after many years of dedicated service.

About the Couple

Richard is a lifelong member of Moore Street Church, having joined as a child. Richard has been very active and has served as finance committee chairman and in many other capacities. He was ordained as deacon in 1984 and continues to serve in that role. Baptized in 1951 at Kehukie Baptist Church, Jean later joined Moore Street and is a member of the Deaconess Board, the Missionaries, and the Senior Group and is active with a health-related support group. Richard and Jean find it gratifying and fulfilling to serve Holy Communion to homebound church members once a month as deacon and deaconess.

Since 1967, Richard has been a Third Degree Mason. He, Jean and family were recognized by Anheuser-Busch and the *Afro American* newspaper when Richard and his family were enrolled in the Families of the Year Honor Roll in 1982. Moore Street Baptist Church also recognized Richard for Outstanding Service to the Finance Committee, 2003. Numerous additional awards have been granted Richard and Waller & Company Jewelers for longevity, integrity, service and commitment to the Richmond community.

Throughout the years, Richard and Jean have had a myriad of interests and hobbies, including gardening, traveling with family and church groups and hosting family gatherings. Reading, drawing, geography and utilizing his artistic skills, along with walking, exercising and keeping up with current events, are also pastimes that give Richard much satisfaction. Jean's other favorite endeavors are shopping/window shopping, collecting themed antiques, cooking delicious meals or dining out. Richard enjoyed membership in

Richmond's Thebans Club, a prestigious men's group started in 1902; and Club 533, a prominent men's social club.

Major events in Richard's and Jean's lives, aside from the births of their sons, Richard III and David, and grandson Alex, included voting for Barack Obama, in 2008 and 2012, the first African American president. Richard and Jean attended the Inaugural Governor's Ball for Lawrence Douglas Wilder, the first African American governor of Virginia. In addition, they witnessed the statue dedication ceremony of Arthur Ashe, who was a Richmond native and an international tennis great. His statue is the first and only one of an African American on Richmond's Monument Avenue. Previously there were only Jim Crow–era statues, which memorialized Virginia Confederate veterans of the Civil War.

Noteworthy celebrations were Richard's and Jean's cruises to the Caribbean for their 25th wedding anniversary and to the Mediterranean for their 50th. Other memorable trips were to Fontana Village, North Carolina; Pipestem State Park, West Virginia; and the World's Fair in Knoxville, Tennessee. In addition, trips with extended Waller kin to The Bahamas, Alaska, and the Dungee Family Reunion in Los Angeles, California, were impressive. They particularly enjoyed Jones Family gatherings, especially homecoming at Jean's home church, Kehukie Baptist, on the third Sunday in August of each year.

Now semi-retired, Richard spends more time enjoying his hobbies and exploring new interests. He is an avid viewer of current national events on TV. He relishes interacting with the public, including his customers, church members, neighbors and new friends. He has earned the community's respect and is sought out for his opinions related to business interests in the downtown Richmond area.

Caring and compassionate, Jean is a loving and supportive wife, mother and grand-mother. She is a very beloved mother-in-law, aunt, sister-in-law and cousin in the Jones and Waller families. She has a great sense of humor and is continually upbeat and encouraging to those who know her. Jean and Richard are very proud of their sons and grandson; all three have completed college, and David, law school.

Richard "Rick" Alexander Waller III

Richard Waller III

Rick was born on July 5, 1963, in Richmond; the firstborn son of Richard Jr. and Jean Jones Waller. As a student, Rick liked sports and excelled in baseball and table tennis. At Jefferson, Huguenot Wythe High School, he played saxophone in the band and lettered all four years in tennis. Also, he won the Future Business Leaders of America Regional Competition and placed second in the Virginia State Competition in 1981. At an early age, Rick began working with his dad in the family jewelry business.

Rick graduated from high school in 1981 and enrolled in Virginia Commonwealth University. There, he joined Alpha Phi Alpha Fraternity Inc., Theta Rho Chapter in 1984. He received a bachelor's degree in business administration and concentration in real estate and minor in psychology, 1994. While at VCU, Rick received a scholarship from the Mid-Atlantic Coca-Cola Bottling Company based on grade point average, leadership abilities and active contributions to the school. He started his landscape business, Premier Landscape, in 1990 while he worked full-time, learning all facets of the family jewelry business. Now Rick successfully operates the firm and is assisted by his dad, Richard Jr.; brother David; and Rick's wife, Kim, along with dedicated employees. Also, Rick has been a Mason in the Silver Trowel Lodge #267 since 2009.

On September 14, 2013, Rick married Kim Lacy, a native of Richmond. Kim is an academician and has earned her Ph.D. degree. She has worked as adjunct professor for Virginia State University and Virginia Commonwealth University in the field of health psychology. Dr. Kim is a deacon at Ebenezer Baptist Church, a member of Zeta Phi Beta Sorority, Inc., and other religious and civic groups. She is the mother of one son, Kenneth Johnson.

Earlier, Rick married Carla Cousins Waller, a native of Victoria, Virginia; and they were blessed with a son, Alex, born on July 13, 1986. Carla and Rick divorced a few years

Kim Waller

later. Sadly, Carla passed away on June 25, 2018, due to a tragic car accident. Alex is a 2012 graduate of Old Dominion University in Norfolk and resides in Charlottesville, Virginia, where he lived as a youth and attended public schools. He joined Alpha Phi Alpha Fraternity, Gamma Alpha Lambda Chapter in 2013. His sports interests are football and basketball. In addition, he likes to cook. Alex is a member of Evergreen Baptist Covenant Church of God in Charlottesville.

David Marcellus Waller

David Waller

David was born February 27, 1971, in Richmond; second son of Richard Jr. and Jean Jones Waller. In elementary school, David played saxophone, represented the city in track and field events and was fifth-grade class vice president. In high school, he excelled in track and field competitions, including running sprints and in high, long and triple jumps. He was an excellent student throughout his school years; he participated in gifted and talented programs and maintained an overall "A" average in his studies.

David began learning the family jewelry business at age eight and often worked at the store on weekends and during the summer. He attended Richmond Community High School, a college prep magnet school, and was one of four valedictorians, Class of 1989. He then attended Hampton University, graduating summa cum laude in 1993 with a major in marketing. At Hampton, David participated in a professional development and internship program, INROADS. Through this program, he interned with Dominion Virginia Power and Wal-Mart. David became counselor for the Leadership, Education and Development Program in Business at Columbia University in New York.

In 1994, David entered Howard University Law School and obtained his juris doctor in 1997. He was then appointed law clerk by the Chief Judge, Superior Court of DC, and clerked for five senior judges. He passed the DC (1998) and Maryland (2000) bar examinations. Since college graduation, David has worked intermittently for the family jewelry company serving as owner-manager. He employs computer inventory and sales systems and creates radio and TV marketing strategies. From 2003 to 2007, he operated a second Waller & Company store at the Virginia Center Commons Mall in Henrico County. David has worked as contract specialist and continues to work in the legal field.

David has a variety of interests, including art and home repair. He honed these skills and applied them to the property he has purchased and manages. At a young age, David spent much time with Mr. Williams, a neighbor who was 50 years older, but a close friend. David is also talented and creative. His art has been exhibited and poetry published citywide in the *American Poetry Anthology*.

**Rick, Richard Jr., David and Jean at a party to celebrate
David's graduation from Hampton U. in 1993**

Richard A. Waller Jr. and Jean Jones Waller Family Pictures

Wedding of Richard and
Jean, December 26, 1959

Richard and Jean and sons
Richard III and David

Richard Jr. and Richard III

Richard Jr. and David

Jean and her siblings. Left to right: Jean,
Doug, Alfreda, Hilda, Morris and Ethel

Jean's parents, Eliza Tootle
Jones and James Jones

Jean's birthplace:
Tootle grandparents'
home, circa 1900

The Wallers' home
in Maymont section
of Richmond

The Wallers' home located
in Richmond's Southside

David, Richard Jr., and Jean at
Richard III's graduation in 1994 from VCU

Celebration time! David graduates from
Howard University Law School, 1997.

David is ecstatic after
his Howard University
graduation in 1997.

Kneeling, Alex; standing: Barbara,
Jean, Joan Cousins (Carla's Mother),
Carla, Rick, David and Richard at
Alex's high school graduation, 2004

Kenneth Johnson Jr. and his
mother, Kim Waller

Carla and son Alex, 2000

The lovely wedding of Dr. Kim Lacy and Richard
A. Waller III. From left: Karen, Thomas Jr. and
Janice Lacy; Kenneth Johnson Jr., Kim and Rick,
Richard IV, Jean, Richard Jr. and David Waller

Wedding happiness:
Richard III and Kim

Kim

Rick, Jean and David

Alex is ready for the
work world, 2012.

Jewel Elizabeth Waller Davis

Jewel and LeCount Davis Sr.

Jewel, Richard and Florence Waller's first baby girl, was born on October 15, 1939. She attended Richmond Public Schools and graduated from Maggie L. Walker High School in 1956. Jewel was an active and involved honor student throughout her school years. Most years beginning about age 12, she worked after school and on Saturdays in the family jewelry shop. After high school, Jewel enrolled at Virginia Union University, where she was a popular student and participated in many aspects of college life. During her sophomore year, she began working in the college's Business Office, filling a position normally held by a full-time employee. In 1958, she was initiated into the Alpha Kappa Alpha Sorority, Inc., Alpha Eta Chapter, and was later elected treasurer and president. She was selected to "Who's Who Among Students in American Universities and Colleges" and voted Miss VUU 1960. She received a Bachelor of Science degree (with honors) in business education in 1961.

Jewel moved to New York City for a few months and worked as a secretary for the New York Housing Authority. One summer prior to graduating, she had also worked in NYC. During both stays, she lived with Aunt Frances' in-laws, Clifton and Arlene Jerome and their daughters. Living in the Harlem section of Manhattan was exciting, but Jewel decided to return to Richmond. Soon, she relocated to Washington, DC, and started her federal career as an accounting technician at the Federal Housing Administration. In 1962, when Jewel entered the federal government, most Blacks were hired in clerical positions at grade levels GS-2 or 3. Jewel was grateful to be employed at GS-5 with an annual salary of about $4,500 (a tiny sum compared to the 2020 starting pay of $33,049 for GS-5).

Her supervisor was LeCount R. Davis, a smart, hardworking accountant and team leader. Jewel excelled in her work and soon left FHA for promotion to GS-7 Personnel Management Specialist at the Internal Revenue Service. She was the first African American female professional in IRS' National Office Personnel. Two years later, she was selected for IRS' prestigious Management Intern Program, becoming the first African American female in that program. Jewel also enrolled at George Washington University at this time and pursued courses in public administration.

While at FHA, Jewel and LeCount became engaged and they were married on June 26, 1965, in a beautiful wedding at Moore Street Church. The Reverend John B. Henderson (Uncle John) performed the ceremony.

Jewel was rapidly promoted at IRS and later transferred to the Office of the Secretary, Department of Transportation. Shortly after moving to Maryland in 1970, she worked for the Food and Drug Administration and the Health Resources and Services Administration, both in the Department of Health and Human Services in Rockville. She was a senior personnel management specialist, managing programs, developing and writing policies, counseling employees and providing technical advice for supervisors and managers. Mother often stated that Jewel was always changing jobs, but during those times, changing agencies was commonplace. Jewel liked the challenge of working in new environments and gaining new experience. In her career, she quickly advanced and received many honors and awards. She left government for a few years and worked as a self-employed personnel management consultant and as assistant to the director of personnel, Montgomery County, Maryland. Following this employment, she returned to the federal workforce before retiring from HRSA in 1997, after 32 years of dedicated service.

LeCount Roscoe Davis Sr.

LeCount was born on August 18, 1937, in Washington, DC, the second of three children born to Henry and Daisy McMillan Davis. LeCount had several older siblings in his blended family and a younger sister, Virginia (Jenny) Davis Fletcher. The two were very close in age and devoted to each other. LeCount played sports with the neighborhood boys club and was a gifted baseball and basketball player. He attended Washington's Armstrong High School and graduated in 1954. His athletic skills led to playing on his high school teams and obtaining a basketball scholarship to Wilberforce University in Wilberforce, Ohio. During the teenage years, LeCount relished dancing and was excellent in Latin American, ballroom and popular dance styles. He and Jenny frequently won dancing contests for their fancy footwork. While in high school, Jenny worked for Mr. Payne, an accountant and tax preparer in their neighborhood. LeCount was interested in Mr. Payne's work and was inspired to pursue a career related to commercial science, accounting and tax planning.

After a year at Wilberforce, LeCount returned home, obtained entry-level positions in the federal government and married. His career started at the Veterans Administration and the Commerce Department's Patent Office. While working full-time, he was also enrolled at Southeastern University, where he graduated in 1960 with bachelor's and master's degrees in commercial science. Later, LeCount transferred to the Federal Housing Administration, progressing to accountant, internal auditor, team leader and supervisory positions.

LeCount was the father of four: LeCount Jr., Garland Antone, Felandria and Michelle Renee. He was a supportive, dedicated and concerned dad. When Jewel and LeCount married, the children lived with them from the ages of eight and ten through college and early adulthood. The six were a family. All the Waller relatives loved and embraced the children. The Davises lived in southwest Washington before moving in 1970 to their beautiful spacious new home at 10600 Crossing Creek Road in Potomac, Maryland. Jewel was devoted to the children and actively involved in their growth and development; nurturing, supporting and guiding them. The youngsters attended area schools: Lake Normandy Elementary, Cabin John Middle and then Churchill High schools, increasing the percentage of African American students enrolled in each school. All participated in various school activities, including the student government, choir, orchestra and sports.

Both the Waller and Davis kinfolk were proud of LeCount and Jewel's move to the new home, where they hosted Christmas dinners, graduation and anniversary parties and numerous special family events. One memorable affair was the family's open house in 1971 celebrating one year in their Potomac residence. The next year, all six Davises traveled to Jamaica in the West Indies for a fun-filled vacation in the sun and sand.

LeCount and Jewel engaged in a host of endeavors involving the youngsters, including parent-teacher associations, football and basketball games, track meets, concerts and more. They were dedicated parents who ensured that their young people had a variety of positive exposures and experiences. Clarinet, piano, dance and drum lessons along with choir and sports practices were the norm around the Davis household. Homework and good grades were a priority. LeCount and Jewel encouraged educational achievement and were extremely proud that all of the children finished Winston Churchill High School and pursued higher education.

Together, they enjoyed concerts, ball games and other fun events; and socialized with family and friends. Garland excelled in sports and was a star athlete from the time he played football with the neighborhood boys club. All the children were members of Suburban Maryland Tots and Teens, and Jewel served as adult leader for the 12- to 14-year-old age group. On Sundays, they attended Mount Calvary Baptist Church.

LeCount was devoted to his mother, Ma Davis; his sister Jenny and her husband, Edward Fletcher; and niece Deborah Jackson Scott. The Davis crew often visited the Fletchers for wonderful cookouts and other gatherings; and Jenny and family frequently visited the Davis home. Both Jenny and Ed were excellent cooks and caterers; on many occasions, they helped LeCount and Jewel entertain, making their joyful events most elegant. In March 2016, after a brief illness, their beloved Jenny passed away.

LeCount was part-time bookkeeper and tax preparer for King Reynolds Certified Public Accounting firm while studying at Southeastern University and working in the government. After leaving the government, LeCount held the position of assistant director of finance at the American Institute for Free Labor Development, a quasi-government agency funded by the U.S. State Department. AIFLD operated in South America and in the Caribbean, and LeCount traveled to many countries in the region. In later years, hotel associations in both Bermuda and The Bahamas engaged LeCount for financial consulting services. He made numerous trips to The Bahamas and often Jewel traveled there with him.

In the mid-1970s, LeCount established his own tax planning and financial management firm, L. R. Davis & Associates. He focused on financial planning to aid clients in their wealth-building and wealth preservation efforts. He prepared for the certified financial planner designation offered by the College for Financial Planning in Denver, Colorado, and received the CFP designation in 1978. LeCount was a trailblazer and the first African American to receive this designation. Jewel was always a key supporter in LeCount's professional endeavors and was proud of this monumental accomplishment, as were all the family.

LeCount, a Registered Investment Advisor in Maryland and an Enrolled IRS agent, has always been enthusiastic about teaching and providing financial advice. In the 1990s to early 2000s, he wrote and published a monthly newsletter, *Finance and the African American Family*; hosted a show, *Common Cents*, on Howard University's television station; and was quoted in various publications. He organized and hosted "The Investors Exchange," a series of financial forums. All of these efforts, along with myriad seminars and workshops he planned and conducted, helped to further the public's knowledge of financial issues. As LeCount has stated over and over, he "wished to impart much of the information and knowledge he gained through his study and his practice."

LeCount's achievements have been recognized as listed:

- Elected president of the local Financial Planning Association, 1980s
- Named "One of the nation's best Financial Planners" by *MONEY* Magazine, 1987
- Received Alpha Kappa Alpha Sorority, Inc., Theta Omega Omega Chapter's Award for Blazing New Trails in Economics, 2000
- Founded the Association of African American Financial Advisors (AAAA), 2001
- Received AAAA's Trailblazer Award, 2006
- Received the International Association for Financial Planning Lifetime Achievement Award, 2008
- Received Montgomery County Section, National Council of Negro Women's Award for Financial Services to the Community, 2015
- Selected for *Investment News'* Lifetime Achievement Excellence in Diversity and Inclusion Award, 2018
- Honored when AAAA established the LeCount R. and Jewel W. Davis Scholarship, 2018
- Recognized as an industry leader by Marquis *Who's Who of Preeminent Innovators and Achievers 2019*
- Received AKA Theta Omega Omega Chapter's Outstanding Community Service Award for Contributions to and Excellence in Building Your Economic Legacy, 2019

LeCount was a member of the Board of Directors and treasurer of Brookland Enterprises, an investment group; and he served on the Board of Advisors of the minority-owned Independence Federal Savings Bank. Also, he was a board member of Social and Scientific Systems, a successful consultant company cofounded by his friend, Herbert J. Miller Sr. For many years, LeCount held membership in the DC men's club Century Limited.

About the Couple

Since retiring from her career in the government in 1997, Jewel has worked for the family's business, Waller & Company Jewelers. In 1998, she established the firm's field service division and was instrumental in expanding the client base and setting up the company's online shopping website. She has been involved in a myriad of efforts to increase the firm's presence in the Washington, Maryland and Northern Virginia region.

Jewel has continued her participation with her beloved sorority, Alpha Kappa Alpha. For over 40 years, she has been an active member of Theta Omega Omega Chapter in Montgomery County. Now a "Golden Soror," she proudly celebrated 50 years of AKA sisterhood and service at the sorority's Centennial Boule in 2008. She is a member of the Emeralds Social Club and has been a longtime financial supporter of VUU. Also, Jewel is a Golden Heritage NAACP member.

In the early 1970s, Jewel joined the Mount Calvary Baptist Church in Rockville and later, LeCount also joined. Jewel has served with the College Care Ministry, the Judah Tribe and in other capacities. LeCount previously chaired the church's Finance Ministry and now leads the Family Financial Literacy Ministry. He regularly attends men's Bible study and is always blessed by attending Mount Calvary's annual men's retreat. In memory of Garland, LeCount and Jewel established a scholarship at MCBC and annually make generous donations to high school graduates entering college. In 2016, LeCount and Jewel donated the initial funding for a new Mount Calvary scholarship set up for students enrolled in college.

Since their honeymoon to Bermuda in 1965, LeCount and Jewel have delighted in traveling. Most memorable were trips to the World's Fair in Canada in 1967, Jamaica in 1971 and The Bahamas. Cruises with family members and friends to the Caribbean, Alaska and Panama; and the Dungee Family Reunion in Hollywood, California, were highlights of their travel experiences. LeCount's and Jewel's many interests during the years include visiting museums and art galleries and collecting art, attending concerts and plays, reading, entertaining and socializing. Listening to a variety of musical genres and following professional sports are also among LeCount's favorite pastimes.

LeCount operated his financial consultation business for over 40 years and is grateful to all of the physicians, small businesses, churches and other clients who utilized his service. Now semi-retired, he continues to actively participate in AAAA and serves as chairman of the AAAA Foundation. LeCount remains passionate about improving financial literacy and helping others. He is a seminar leader and mentors individuals in the financial services industry; many younger African American professionals consider him "The Godfather of Financial Planning." In early 2020, LeCount published his memoirs in the volume *One Step Back - Two Steps Forward.*

Jewel and LeCount have had the love and support of family members and numerous friends, including Jewel's childhood pal Shirley Jefferson Logan, who departed this life in April 2019, and her husband, Lawrence. The Logans named LeCount and Jewel as godparents of their first child, Monique. Voyce and Katie Whitley, LeCount's and Jewel's "big brother and big sister," have been great friends since the early 1970s while active with Tots and Teens. The couples have enjoyed traveling, attending parties and celebrating anniversaries and other events.

Jewel's bridal photo

Jewel is thoughtful, caring, generous and well organized. Her concern for others and her giving spirit have been exhibited in a variety of ways throughout her life. She is blessed to live a life of service and sacrifice with much faith and trust in God. She is thankful to be a positive role model and a confident Black woman, like her beloved mother and Aunt May, both of whom she greatly admired and sorely misses.

In 2010, LeCount and Jewel moved to their new condominium home in Potomac and continue to enjoy their favorite endeavors. On June 26, 2020, they celebrated 55 years of marriage. They appreciate the love, happiness and respect they share. To God be the glory.

LeCount Davis Jr.

LeCount Roscoe Davis Jr.

LeCount Jr. was born on January 29, 1957, the first child of LeCount and Ruth Tolson Davis. LeCount was an honor roll student through his years in the DC and Montgomery County schools. He was a talented musician, who took clarinet lessons for a number of years and enjoyed playing the instrument as a member of the DC Youth Orchestra and his high school orchestra. He also sang in the school choir and was an outstanding swimmer. LeCount excelled academically at Churchill High and was offered numerous scholarships upon graduation in 1975.

His choice of colleges was Peabody Conservatory of Music in Baltimore and he planned to study music. However, he changed his focus and enrolled at the University of California, Berkeley. Later, LeCount moved to Paris, France, and studied there before returning to the U.S. and enrolling in Middlebury College in Middlebury, Vermont. He graduated from the college with bachelor's and master's degrees in French civilization. LeCount has worked for many years for a Washington, DC–based consulting firm and has been assigned to various management projects at the National Institutes of Health in Bethesda, Maryland.

Garland Antone Davis

Garland was born on February 11, 1959, the second child of LeCount and Ruth Tolson Davis. He had a gregarious personality and was a gifted athlete. Garland played sports for the neighborhood boys club while in elementary and junior high schools. At Churchill High, he excelled in football, basketball and track; and received many honors and awards for his achievements. Garland spoke Spanish fluently and took

Garland Davis

drum lessons. An active member of Suburban Maryland Tots and Teens, Garland enjoyed playing drums for many of the group's special programs.

In 1977, Garland graduated from Churchill and was awarded a football scholarship to attend West Texas State University in Canyon, Texas. There, he was a good student and a standout wide receiver on the team. Garland earned a bachelor's degree in accounting in 1981. Afterwards, he was employed as an auditor for the Dallas School System. Garland was extremely social and personable and was loved by all. In 1991, at age 32, Garland passed away in Tucson, Arizona, in a train accident. His untimely death at this young age was devastating for all the family and friends.

Felandria "Fele" Davis Coles

Felandria Davis Coles

Felandria was born on August 21, 1960, the first daughter of LeCount and Ruth Tolson Davis. Fele enjoyed spending time with her cousins, other family members and her friends. She liked to sing and was a member of Churchill High School's choir and Mount Calvary Baptist Church's youth choir, utilizing her musical talents to sing show tunes, popular music and songs of praise.

In 1978, Felandria graduated from Churchill and enrolled at Morgan State University, where she studied for two years. Later, she attended Strayer College.

Fele attended sports events and was active in Tots and Teens. She relished participating in special Tots and Teens programs and in various group outings. Ice skating and bowling were among her favorite activities. As teenagers, both she and her sister Michelle babysat for families living in the neighborhood. She married and lives in the Washington area. Currently, Fele's preferred pastimes are playing tennis and singing.

Michelle Renee Davis Martin

Michelle Davis Martin

Michelle Renee was born July 10, 1961, the second daughter of LeCount and Ruth Tolson Davis. Michelle was an honor roll student who participated in many school activities and was on Churchill's track team. She was an ardent fan of Garland's and attended all of his games, along with family members. Michelle enjoyed Tots and Teens events, had many friends in the group and was eager to participate in the club's outings, cultural events and special programs.

Michelle finished Churchill in 1979. She then entered the College of William and Mary in Williamsburg, Virginia, and graduated in 1983 with a bachelor's degree in sociology. At William and Mary, Michelle met her future husband, Hansen O. Martin, also a graduate of the college. They were married on July 10, 1985, in a beautiful ceremony at Mount Calvary Baptist Church.

The family lived in Fort Huachuca, Arizona, and in other locations while Hansen was in the military. After his military service, the Martins lived in Woodbridge, Virginia, before moving to Richmond in more recent years. Michelle and Hansen are the parents of three children, Hansen Jr., Laura and Danielle; and the grandparents of a baby boy. All are actively engaged in religious efforts and spend much time with church-related services and events.

Jewel Waller Davis and
LeCount R. Davis Family Pictures

June 26, 1965, wedding portrait of Jewel and LeCount
From left: Jean Marie Waller, Joyce W. Baden, Jewel, LeCount, Virginia Davis,
Barbara Young and Shirley Logan; Flower girls: daughters of Cynthia Brown and
Nessa Johnson; Ring bearer: Kevin Johnson, son of Ernest and Adele Johnson

Richard and Jewel

**Our mother
was elegant**

**The newlyweds honeymoon
in Bermuda, 1965.**

Jewel in 1954

A treasured keepsake, Jewel's last birthday
card from Mother and Daddy in 1955

Jewel is "1960 Miss
Virginia Union U."

Jewel, "Career Girl"
IRS Intern, 1965

Jewel with fellow Charmerettes Social Club
members at a 1954 Gala. What a charming
and elegant group of teens!

Jewel and LeCount
celebrate their first year
in their new home, 1971.

LeCount and his sister,
Virginia Davis Fletcher

Michelle, Garland,
LeCount Jr. and Felandria

Our Potomac home for 39 years. A source
of much pride and many happy memories

LeCount, Jewel and the children,
Christmas at Joyce's, 1978

LeCount's sister, Virginia Fletcher, 1990s; Mother, Daisy
"Ma" Davis, 1970s; and niece, Deborah Scott, 2010

LeCount, Michelle and Jewel on Michelle's wedding day, August 1985

Sisters Michelle and Felandria on Michelle's wedding day

LeCount—A trailblazer, first African American Certified Financial Planner Designation conferred 1978

Jewel receives an award from Sec. of US Department of Transportation, John Volpe, in the 1970s.

LeCount, 2000

Jewel, 1990s

LeCount and Jewel on an
Alaskan Cruise, 2008

In 2008, Living Life Like It's Golden:
50-Year AKA Celebration; Mary McLean,
Beulah Jackson, Mattie Carey and Jewel

Jewel and cousin Jean at a
Richmond Gala, 1990s

LeCount and Jewel's Caribbean cruise
with Voyce and Katie Whitley, 1990s

Stepping out for a
fabulous evening, 1980s

Joyce Dungee Waller Baden

Aubrey Jr. and Joyce Baden

Joyce was born on December 31, 1942, in Richmond and was the second daughter of Richard and Florence Waller. At age three, Joyce moved to Norfolk and eventually became the foster daughter of her uncle and aunt, the Reverend John B. and Lillian D. Henderson.

Joyce was enrolled in Norfolk Public Schools and completed Booker T. Washington High School in 1959. She received a bachelor's degree in physics from Norfolk State College with honors in 1963. While a student at NSU, Joyce was initiated as a charter member of Delta Sigma Theta Sorority, Inc., Epsilon Theta Chapter. In the fall of 1963, she taught mathematics at Union-Kempsville High School in Virginia Beach, where she met Elvin and Roy Reid, now lifelong friends. One year later, Joyce went to Washington, enrolled in Howard University's graduate school, and met Aubrey Garcia Baden Jr., of Annapolis. The Baden and Henderson families' mutual friend, Joseph Wallace Brown, a native of Annapolis and registrar at Norfolk State, vouched for Aubrey and Joyce's integrity to their prospective in-laws!

On May 28, 1965, Aubrey and Joyce were married by Uncle John at Bank Street Baptist Church. It was a small wedding, attended by Aunt May; Mother; Aubrey's parents, Garcia and Sophronia Baden; Wallace Brown and Rosa Robinson, a family friend. In September, Aunt May and Uncle John gave the couple a wondrous wedding reception in Norfolk with nearly 200 guests. After marrying, Aubrey and Joyce lived in Annapolis.

Two weeks prior to their marriage, Joyce was interviewed for employment by Illinois Institute of Technology Research Institute (IITRI) and after discussing her skills, she talked about her impending marriage to Aubrey, his academic record, and that he was to be interviewed by IITRI in the following week. When Aubrey reported to the company for his short and positive interview, his evaluators said that they knew about his skills from Joyce. That very afternoon, he and Joyce received job offers. Immediately following their marriage, they reported for work at IITRI of Chicago, at the Annapolis facility that housed one of its science and engineering divisions. Joyce and Aubrey were employed by IITRI's Electromagnetic Compatibility Analysis Center. Soon after becoming employed, they were able to purchase a home in the Bestgate section of Annapolis.

Joyce and Aubrey were blessed with their treasured son, Aubrey Garcia III. He was born on December 13, 1967. Joyce worked at IITRI until Aubrey was born; and for nearly two years afterwards, she did not work full-time. She was at home and gained all of the pleasure of being with their baby.

Beginning in 1969, Joyce was employed by Maryland state government in a variety of agencies as information systems management specialist until she retired in 1996. For her last 14 years, she worked at the Maryland Higher Education Commission (MHEC). During her tenure at MHEC, she returned to school and completed a master's degree in management at the University of Maryland University College in 1987.

Aubrey Garcia Baden Jr.

Aubrey was born on May 19, 1938, in Annapolis, Maryland, only son of Aubrey Sr. and Helen Sophronia Baden. He attended Stanton Elementary School and Wiley H. Bates High School; he graduated in 1956, as part of a fantastic class! During his younger years, he liked fishing, basketball and billiards. Aubrey has always had an interest in science and is a "sidewalk astronomer." At the age of 16, he built his first telescope.

Prepared with a Bachelor of Science in physics from Morgan State University in 1960, he completed additional studies at Howard and Johns Hopkins Universities. From 1961 to 1964, he served in the U.S. Army with the VII Corps Artillery Headquarters in Germany. Aubrey continued working at IITRI, a government military contractor, as software engineer in numerous positions until his retirement in 1995, after 30 years of service.

His was a very large family that included his parents, his loving and faithful sister Angela Baden Howard, grandparents, and other familial connections. He has a niece, Wendy Howard, and a nephew, Daniel Howard III, and many close and affectionate cousins.

Aubrey was nominated in 1994 by IITRI for the Black Engineer of the Year Award. Director John Scott presented Aubrey a citation in 1995 "for dedication to the objectives of IITRI at the Joint Spectrum Center and the use of your expertise to achieve its goals."

Aubrey has indicated that his most ardent desire is for more people of color to choose to study science, technology, engineering and math disciplines in the future.

About the Couple

Aubrey and Joyce's early and middle years in Annapolis were chock-full with work, parenting, Aubrey III's activities, visits with family, and church worship and events. Holidays and other special occasions were most often shared with kin and close friends. Those were wonderful and memorable times. Museum trips, attending concerts, theater and dance productions, shopping and lunching with chums also were happy experiences for Joyce. Later, during their parents' more mature years, Joyce, Aubrey and Aubrey III assisted Aunt May, Mother and Daddy Garcia.

Joyce was confirmed in 1974 at St. Philip's Episcopal Church and has served as a member of the choir, Episcopal Church Women and on innumerable ad hoc committees. She has worked as church school superintendent and teacher, and in other facets of church life. She has volunteered with Habitat for Humanity; NAACP Anne Arundel County; as co-leader of a Brownie troop and Delta Sigma Theta Sorority, Annapolis Alumnae Chapter. She is a life member of the NAACP.

Aubrey is a lifetime member of St. Philip's Church. During many of these years he had varied responsibilities: he taught Sunday School, worked with the Finance Committee and was a member of the Vestry. Also, Aubrey volunteered for Habitat for Humanity and the Anne Arundel County NAACP Education Committee. Several years after his retirement, he became a USUI SHIKI RYOHO Reiki Master. (Reiki is a form of alternative medicine called energy healing.)

He relishes gardening, carpentry, reading, travel, entertaining and visiting outdoor scenic locations and zoos. He developed an interest in carpentry and has made renovations to their home. His interest in astronomy and space exploration, which began when he was a teenager, continues. As an adult, Aubrey purchased a large telescope, and for many years, he called neighbors to view various astronomical events.

The family has had many exciting vacations. They traveled to Disney World with Aubrey III and Aunt May in 1976. Later, they made trips to California and the Mexican Riviera. Cruises and trips were made even more special because kin and friends traveled with Joyce and Aubrey. These included adventures to The Bahamas, Bermuda, New

England, Alaska, Panama, Grand Canyon and Las Vegas. Joyce and Aubrey III's 13-day excursion to Spain and Portugal in 1988 was extraordinary. The holiday spent in Paris, with friends Jane Libby, Aliceteen Mangum and Joan McCullough, was the ultimate escape and the fulfillment of Joyce's lifetime dream.

Aubrey and Joyce are thankful to God for His countless blessings: their long marriage of 55 years, their cherished son, incredible parents and other relatives, and exceptionally caring brother, sisters, sisters-in-law and brothers-in-law. They are appreciative of their supportive church family, neighbors, friends and brilliant work colleagues. Aubrey and Joyce have been enriched by those relationships and are grateful for them. They especially miss their beloved parents: Daddy (1955), Uncle John (1974), Mother Sophronia (1984), Aunt May (1987), Mother Florence (1993) and Daddy Garcia (2001).

Aubrey and Joyce value higher education and are gratified to make a small donation each year to a scholarship fund they established at Virginia Union University in memory of Aunt May and Uncle John, and to the foundations at Morgan State and Norfolk State. All of these institutions are Historically Black Colleges and Universities (HBCUs).

"For I know the plans I have for you, declares the LORD, plans to prosper you and not to harm you, plans to give you hope and a future." Jeremiah 29:11.

Aubrey Garcia Baden III

Aubrey Baden III

Aubrey III, the only child and son of Aubrey and Joyce, and a profound blessing to them, was born December 13, 1967, in Annapolis, Maryland. He had as his daycare provider Mrs. Callie Barge Johnson, who was beloved and like a member of the family. Beginning at about age 10, and for many years thereafter, Aubrey created fictional characters and wrote hundreds of plays about them. He graduated from the Queen Anne School in Upper Marlboro, Maryland, in 1986, where he received a number of academic awards, as well as the Drew Tidler Award for character. Aubrey then enrolled at St. Mary's College of Southern Maryland (SMCM); his scriptwriting was a factor in his receiving a full-tuition scholarship. Aubrey earned a Bachelor of Arts (Language and Literature) from SMCM in 1990, with honors. After two years of employment, he matriculated at the University of Maryland, College Park, and obtained a master's degree in English in 1994. Aubrey continued postgraduate studies there for an additional two years.

He has taught in Maryland as follows: C. E. Smith Jewish Day School, Rockville; Spaulding Catholic High School, Gambrills; Sojourner-Douglass College, Annapolis; and Broadneck Senior High School, 2004–2017, Annapolis. Aubrey currently teaches English at Anne Arundel Community College, Arnold, where he is gratified to nurture students' critical-thinking skills.

A lifetime member of Saint Philip's Episcopal Church, he was confirmed in 1979 and has served as lector, chorister and counter, and assists with volunteer efforts. Aubrey's special passion is attending and participating in theatrical performances. As an adult, he has performed in more than 30 local theater productions at various venues, including the Annapolis Summer Garden, Colonial Players, Merely Players and Second Star theaters; and has sung with the Annapolis Chorale and Saint Philip's Episcopal Church choir. He has a great musical "ear." His perfect pitch has served him well in his performances in musical theater and in various choral pursuits.

He was dearly loved by all of his doting grandparents. Daddy Garcia and Mommy Phronie took him to dine out with them weekly before he began school. He often visited with Aunt May and Uncle John in Norfolk; they purchased Aubrey's NAACP Junior Life Membership before he was age two! Aubrey spent a great deal of time with Mother Florence when she stayed with Joyce; he recalls many of her stories about the past and about Grandfather Richard. Aubrey is outgoing and compassionate, and he knows how to engage with folk of all ages, ethnicities and interests. His parents are gratified to have witnessed Aubrey achieve many of his goals.

Aubrey maintains connections with kin and has an astounding memory of their special occasions; he reminds them of their events and has written poems to commemorate celebrations. He exhibits great devotion to his parents and other family; and was kindhearted to his grandparents. Aubrey is indebted to people of color of older generations who have paved the way for him to engage in theater and other community activities. He states, "Race should not be a deterrent for pursuing one's passions and goals."

Joyce Waller Baden and Aubrey G. Baden Jr. Family Pictures

Wedding Day,
May 28, 1965

Wedding Day, May 28, 1965
Mother, Aubrey, Uncle John, Joyce and Aunt May

Wedding Reception,
September 1965

Aubrey Jr.'s
grandparents, William
and Ethel Banks
Chapman, 1967

Aubrey Jr.'s parents,
Aubrey G. Sr. and Helen
Sophronia Baden, 1970s

Aunt May and Uncle John, 1960s

Aubrey's nephew and niece, Daniel
III and Wendy Howard; Aubrey
III, Aubrey Jr., Angela Baden,
Aubrey Sr. and Joyce, late 1980s

Mother holding Aubrey III, 1968

Mrs. Callie Johnson, loving family friend

Aubrey ages 1 to 8 years

Seated: Aubrey III, Joyce, Aubrey Sr., Sophronia and Aunt May. Standing: Uncle John and Aubrey Jr., December 1968

Aunt May and Uncle John, mid-1960s

Mother and Aubrey at his graduation from St. Mary's College May 1990

Aubrey sings at St. Philip's Episcopal Church, 2017

Aubrey in the play *Whose Cross Is It?*

John Scott presents Aubrey with a 25-Year Service Award from IITRI, 1990

Colleagues celebrate Aubrey just before his retirement in 1995; about 40 of his work colleagues wore flannel shirts, as he often did.

Aubrey and Joyce at a Poconos, Pennsylvania, resort in 1987

Aubrey and Joyce on a night out

Joyce photographed her BFFs going out for a fun day! Andrea Parham, Aliceteen Mangum, Natalie Ballard, Nancy Johnson, Barbara Nealy and Cynthia Crowner, 1991

Several more of Joyce's friends: Nancy Johnson, Margo Offer, Joyce, Jeanette Thomas and Fredericka Tubaya

Lillian "Lill" Fannie Regina Waller Thomas Moore

Haywood and Lillian Moore

Lillian was born on July 8, 1944, and was the third daughter of Richard and Florence Waller. She attended Richmond Public Schools and transferred to Booker T. Washington in Norfolk for her last two years of high school. She graduated from there in 1962.

Lillian then moved to Washington, DC, and was employed at Providence Hospital, where she met her future husband, Robert Earl Thomas. Lillian and Robert were married in 1963 and are the proud parents of two sons: Robert Earl Jr. and Rodney Erik. Lillian later worked at Sears Roebuck and Company and in other retail sales positions. At Sears, she met Katie Williams Cox Johnson, who became her best friend and their friendship has remained through the years. In 1971, Robert and Lillian were divorced; she became a single mother. She was employed at Riggs National Bank as a processing teller and purchased her first home.

She studied at Washington Technical Institute to become a nursing assistant. She was awarded an associate degree in nursing, completing a program that led to the registered nursing degree from Prince George's Community College in 1975. Lillian passed her nursing boards exams, fulfilling her dream to become a registered nurse. Around this time, Lillian and her sons moved to Richmond, her beloved hometown, where she worked for several months as a graduate nurse at McGuire Veterans Hospital. After a while, the family returned to the DC area and lived in Silver Spring, Maryland, prior to moving back to Washington. She was employed at DC General Hospital, General Medicine Unit. Lillian was in that position for four years before transferring to the hospital's Medical Follow-Up Clinic and working there for eight years. It was at DC General Hospital that Lillian met George, a native of Ponce, Puerto Rico. The two would soon marry.

Lill continued her service as a registered nurse at various hospitals. She had a fulfilling career and for years functioned as a case management review nurse at Prince George's Community Hospital in Cheverly, Maryland. Lill retired from Prince George's in 2012.

Throughout her long tenure as a nurse, she was intensely dedicated to and concerned for the health and well-being of the innumerable patients who were in her care.

Haywood Moore

Haywood "George" Ortice Moore

Haywood was born on October 22, 1930, the son of Mrs. Tinney Funderburk and Mr. Moore, a merchant marine from Panama. Lillian and George were joined in holy matrimony on May 26, 1979. George had been married previously and was the father of Perez and Carmelita Aughtry; Conchita Moore (deceased 2018), Lopez Moore (deceased 2013), Manuel Moore and Carmen Moore Montue.

George was reared in Washington, DC, and received his early education in Catholic schools, followed by his enrollment at Shaw Junior High School, then at Armstrong High School. Later, he studied electronics at the University of the District of Columbia. As a young boy, he spent time with his uncles and aunts in Philadelphia and was happy to return home during the baseball season. He assisted his mother at the neighborhood grocery store that she owned and helped his stepfather work on cars. George's early interest in cars led to a lifetime hobby of collecting and restoring Mercedes-Benz and other brands of automobiles. Also, in his younger years, George acquired martial arts skills; the family has a wonderful painting of him in karate attire.

From 1949 to 1950, George was employed as a pipe threader with the United Clay Company of Washington. In 1950, he enlisted in the all-Black U.S. Army, 82nd Airborne Division in Washington and received basic training at Fort Bragg, North Carolina. He spoke often about his military experiences, and especially about his parachute training with the 82nd Division Jump School and a major course, Basic Airborne, which he completed in 1951. His most significant duty assignment was CIR Co 307th Medical Battalion, Airborne. He received an honorable discharge on October 4, 1953, ending his military service with excellent new skills, as he had completed x-ray technician training in the U.S. Army Medical Service. Afterward, George worked as a painter at DC Village and received outstanding ratings and awards before retiring in 1990 after 36 years of dedicated service.

About the Couple

George and Lill were a happy and loving couple, who had many interests and lived life to the fullest. They were involved in the Longview Community in Saint Mary's County, Maryland, where they owned a summer home and had made a number of friends. The two invited their kin to visit and spend weekends. Both were members of Longview's Community Recreation Association and assisted in planning holiday festivities and other events.

On weekends, when the weather was favorable, the couple set up tables at an outdoor market in Saint Mary's County, where they displayed and sold a variety of accessories for women and men. George's son, Manuel, usually assisted them. Lillian was a successful and expert salesperson and exhibited her entrepreneurial skills as she participated in this business that she and George established.

She was very creative and talented as well. Lill collected cookbooks and experimented with new recipes, preparing many special dishes for her family. For years, Lill and George enjoyed visiting the Adams-Morgan area of DC for the festive Latin American music and food. When halo hats were trending, Lill liked to make this style of hat and sold them to her friends. Lill and George entertained kin often in their beautifully decorated home. At one time, Lill's decorating theme was "cats," and she found many imaginative ways to enhance their home's ambience by artfully displaying her fanciful collection of ceramic, metal and wooden cats and feline-themed artifacts.

Lillian joined Gethsemane Baptist Church in Washington in the early 1980s. For a number of years, she sang with the senior choir and attended Adult Bible Class #1 each Sunday. Lillian was an active member of the Missionaries and the Tribe of Benjamin. In 2010, George was baptized at Gethsemane by the Reverend Khalfani Drummer and joined Lillian in volunteering with the Missionaries. They both were especially gratified when ministering to residents of the Stoddard Baptist Home, which they visited regularly. Often Lill delivered the inspirational message at these devotional services. Also, George and Lill frequently prepared and distributed sandwiches and necessities to the homeless. On numerous occasions, they provided warm socks and gloves in the cold winter months. They were a generous couple, who always thought of others.

Lill worked diligently in her neighborhood. While living on Webster Street, she organized the Block Club and joined the Northwest Boundary Civic Association; and while a resident of Allison Street in Northeast, she served as secretary of the Queens Chapel Civic Association. Sometime in the 1970s, Lill became a member of Eta Phi Beta Sorority and for several years, she and George often participated with Mother in various Richmond chapter events.

Beginning in 2004, Manuel resided with Lillian and George on Allison Street and was an integral part of their family. He joined them in most of their activities. In early 2017, as Lill's health deteriorated, a guardian was appointed for Manuel and he moved to another residence.

Lillian and George enjoyed travel, international and domestic, often traveling with family members. A favorite destination was Detroit to visit Lillian's disabled friend, Gladys. Lillian's first flight was in 1978 with George, Robert and Rodney to visit Disneyland, Los Angeles, Las Vegas and San Francisco. George and Lillian flew to San Juan and Ponce, Puerto Rico, in the early 1980s. They traveled to Ansbach, Germany, to visit Rodney while he was stationed there. Additionally, George and Lillian toured Paris, France, and London, England, in the mid-1980s. They relished these trips as well as excursions to the Caribbean Islands and Canada. Their last major trip was a Bahamian cruise in 2013 with Rodney and wife Lena, Manuel, and six of Lillian's and George's grandchildren. In addition to traveling, George's special interests included boating, fishing, playing conga drums, dancing and listening to Latin American music.

George was devoted to Lill and he did all he could to please her and their family. He and our mother had a singular relationship; he was caring and spent many hours with her when she visited him and Lill. George could repair almost anything and assisted Mother and others with painting and various repairs. Well-liked by his work colleagues, neighbors and church family, he was an engaging conversationalist. He was tall, handsome and had an imposing presence. George took great pride in his appearance and was always very smartly dressed.

George was a dedicated and loving father, stepfather, grandfather and uncle who made time for the younger generation and shared his wisdom with them. Lillian was a very devoted grandmother and was forever eager to spend time with the grandchildren. Whenever the youngsters were in Lill's and George's presence, the grandparents were joyful and happy. Anything the "grands" desired, Lill and George wanted to furnish for their beloved Kweisi, Hasani, Sequoia, Dakari, Noelle, Aaliyah, Amaya and Adrian. She and George loved them deeply.

After Lillian retired from her nursing career, she provided special and loving care for George at home for a few years during his illness and before he was hospitalized. The year 2018 became a very difficult one for the Waller family. George was called home to be with our Lord and Savior on March 10, 2018, while a patient at the Veterans Administration Hospital in Washington, DC. He was much loved and is sorely missed by his relatives and friends. A beautiful celebration of his life was held on March 16, 2018. A few weeks later, on May 4, 2018, his daughter Conchita died suddenly.

Following George's demise, our beloved sister Lillian's health declined. A few months after entering a facility, she was hospitalized several times before passing away on December 18, 2018, at Doctors Hospital in Lanham, Maryland. Her life was celebrated by all the family and numerous church members and friends at Gethsemane Baptist Church on December 27, 2018. Her interment was in the family plot at Fort Lincoln Cemetery in Bladensburg, Maryland, next to her beloved George. Lillian was much loved and respected, and all greatly miss her loving spirit. May Lillian, George and his deceased children rest in perfect peace.

Lillian and George's fondest dream was to build a well in an African country to provide clean water. In memory of Lillian and George, a water catchment system was installed at LWanda Secondary and Primary Schools in Kenya.

Robert "Rob" Earl Thomas Jr.

Robert Thomas Jr.

Robert was born on November 14, 1963, in Washington, and is the first son of Robert Earl Thomas and Lillian Waller Thomas Moore. He is the stepson of Haywood "George" Moore and Sallie Dixon Thomas. Robert completed his elementary and secondary education in DC public schools and received his high school diploma from Roosevelt High School, graduating in 1981. He attended Norfolk State College for two years and later enrolled in courses at the University of the District of Columbia.

Rob was employed by the American Council of Life Insurance and worked as assistant service manager at Community Computers. Rob's interest in management, finance and business led him to establish Scrubnik Lawncare, Inc. in 1987. Initially, the undertaking was instituted as a partnership; however, Rob later became sole proprietor. He utilized his extensive entrepreneurial and management skills to obtain numerous federal and local government and residential contracts; he employed many workers to fulfill these contractual obligations. For over 30 years, Rob successfully operated Scrubnik Lawncare before retiring in 2018.

In 1997, Robert married Olatungi "Tungi" Jones-Dove, a native of Sierra Leone, West Africa. Two beautiful children were born to this union: son Kweisi Robert, born February 2, 1999; and daughter Sequoia Olatungi, born November 7, 2000. Some time prior to marrying, Rob had purchased a beautiful home in Avondale, Maryland, and the family enjoyed living near his mother, Lillian. After a few years in this home, Rob and Tungi bought a spacious new residence in Beltsville, Maryland. Rob and Tungi were later divorced.

Rob was baptized at Gethsemane Baptist Church in Washington and served on its Board of Trustees and in other roles. His favorite pastimes are gardening, expanding his knowledge of computer technology, listening to gospel and rhythm and blues music and coin collecting (numismatics).

Rob is extremely proud of his children. Son Kwesi graduated from Arundel High School in 2017. He immediately joined the U.S. Marine Corps and currently serves with the Marines in various locations. Sequoia is a 2019 graduate of Arundel High and now attends Anne Arundel Community College. She plans to enroll at Towson State University and study cybersecurity.

In 2009, Rob and Rodney mourned the loss of their much-loved younger brother, Ronald, son of Robert and Sallie Thomas. Through the years, Rob and Rodney remained close to Ronald; their father, Robert Earl; and their stepmother, Sallie. Both sons were fond of their stepfather, George, and devoted to their mother, Lillian, with whom they shared a distinct connection. George died in March of 2018 and Lillian passed away in December of 2018; their deaths were a profound loss to Rob and his children.

For the Wallers, the year 2020 has been an exceptional one for weddings, when a niece, a nephew and a grand-nephew married. On March 25, Ta-Tianna and Chris McFadden wed. In the fall of 2020, Kweisi, who was stationed at a military base in California, announced his marriage to Kasachi Richardson, a native of St. Louis, Missouri. Kasachi is the mother of Kirin, a delightful little 3-year-old girl, who immediately won her grandfather Rob's heart. The newlyweds met many Waller and Thomas family members when they visited the Maryland area for a brief while.

Shortly before Christmas, on December 18, 2020, Cupid's arrow struck again, when Rob and Patricia "Patty" Finney were married. Patty, a native of Easton, Maryland, is the daughter of Willie Lee Finney and Willie May Finney. Patty has two adult children: Dimesha Johnson and De'neco Garcia, and is the grandmother of three. Patty is warm and personable; she brings a smile and joy to Rob and to all who know her. Due to the pandemic, family members and friends witnessed Rob's and Patty's ceremony by means of a teleconference. The Rev. Dr. Khalfani Drummer, pastor of Gethsemane Baptist Church in Washington, DC, officiated.

All relatives and friends of the newlyweds wish them God's blessings. Here is our toast to the three newly married couples:

In life, God gives us many blessings but the greatest one of all is love. What are we without it? Nothing. And so, by having each other's unwavering love, they have everything. We all toast to the love that these couples share.

Robert Thomas and Patty Finney Thomas

Rodney Erik Thomas

Evalena and Rodney Thomas

Rodney was born on August 24, 1966, in Washington, DC, and is the second son of Robert Earl Thomas Sr. and Lillian Waller Thomas Moore. He is the stepson of Haywood "George" Moore and Sallie Dixon Thomas.

Rodney attended DC public schools and graduated from Calvin Coolidge High School in 1984. He enlisted in the U.S. Army in September of that year. After his military service, Rodney enrolled at the University of the District of Columbia and graduated with a bachelor's degree in English in 1992. He pursued graduate education and earned the Master of Business Administration (MBA) degree in June 1998 from Howard University.

Rodney's career includes work as a program analyst at Mitchell Systems,1990 to 1993; and at KPMG Peat Marwick LLP, 1993 to 1996. In 1996 he and KPMG coworker Deana Herbert founded Thomas & Herbert Consulting (T&H) LLC. Their very successful management consulting firm delivers management and IT consulting services. Rodney, chairman and CEO, has led the company's phenomenal growth, winning contracts from federal, state and local government entities.

He is author of the book *Federal Government Reengineering: Truth or Dare?* T&H is notably generous and provides food and gifts for needy families during the Thanksgiving and Christmas seasons.

In 1992, Rodney married Elizabeth Nataly Garcia, a Washington, DC, native of Dominican descent. Two sons were born to this union: Hasani Erik, June 16, 2000, and Dakari Marcel, April 17, 2003. The couple was divorced in 2007. Rodney is also the father of Noelle Laila, born July 14, 2008, daughter of Rodney and Tanya Miller. As a baby, Noelle was blessed at her great-aunt Jewel's and great-uncle LeCount's church, Mount Calvary Baptist in Rockville.

Rodney married Evalena "Lena" Ford, a Virginia native and daughter of David Aaron Ford, on October 14, 2012, in the exquisite gardens of the Gramercy Mansion in Baltimore, Maryland. From this union, Rodney gained a stepdaughter, Aaliyah Chanel

Foster, Lena's daughter, who was born on July 11, 2008. Rodney and Lena were blessed with baby Amaya Leilani, born on September 2, 2014. Rodney has one grandson, Adrian Miguel Thomas, born June 2, 2017, son of Hasani Erik.

The family attends Gethsemane Baptist Church in Washington, where Rodney was baptized a number of years ago and where Hasani and Dakari were baptized. Rodney is also a supporter of the Fishing School in Washington. He enjoys cross-fit exercise, including a blend of spinning bikes, weight lifting, treadmill, elliptical and other types of exercise.

T&H and Rodney have received numerous awards as listed below:

- The U.S. Department of Agriculture Rural Development named T&H Veterans-Owned Small Business of the Year, 2015.
- *Washington SmartCEO GovStar* Technical listed T&H as a Trailblazer, Medium category, 2011.
- Diversity Business.com selected T&H as one of the top 500 minority-owned businesses in the nation, 2006–2010.
- Rodney was named one of the 25 Most Powerful Minority Men in Business by the Minority Enterprise Executive Council, 2008.
- *Government VAR Magazine* cited T&H as Small Business Solutions Provider of the Year and placed Rodney's photo on the magazine's cover, 2007.
- *Washington Technology* Fast 50 ranked T&H as one of the 50 fastest-growing small government IT companies in the nation, in 2005 and 2006.
- Maryland Top 100 ranked T&H as one of the fastest-growing and most admired small or minority-owned companies in the state of Maryland, 2006.
- *Inc.* 500 cited T&H as one of the fastest-growing companies in the nation, 2004 and 2005.
- T&H received the Washington Technology Champions Award; and Maryland Governor Robert Erlich named T&H one of the leading technology companies in Maryland, 2005.
- The Department of Homeland Security recognized T&H for exemplary performance on the DHS Terrorist Watchlist Project, 2004.
- T&H received the DHS Mentor-Protégé Performance Award along with its mentor, Bearing Point (now Deloitte), 2004.

Rodney and Lena spend considerable time with a myriad of activities involving the children's sports and other events. Noelle and Amaya play soccer, Aaliyah plays lacrosse and Dakari plays basketball. Hasani was an excellent swimmer and now engages in other sports. The family relishes traveling, deep-sea fishing, hiking, skiing, biking and bowling. Other favorite interests include dining out, watching movies at their in-home theater room and attending shows, plays and concerts.

All the children have achieved in school and are making their parents proud. Hasani is a student at Montgomery College in Takoma Park, Maryland, and is majoring in business. Dakari is a senior at Walter Johnson High School and plans to enroll in college after graduation in 2021. Currently, Noelle attends Southern Maryland Christian Academy and is a straight "A" student. Aaliyah attends North Bethesda Middle School in Bethesda, where she is an honor student. Amaya completed her last year at Georgetown Hill in Potomac and will be attending Wyngate Elementary School in the fall of 2020.

In 2009, Rob and Rodney mourned the loss of their much-loved younger brother, Ronald, son of Robert and Sallie Thomas. Through the years, Rob and Rodney remained close to Ronald; their father Robert Earl; and their stepmother, Sallie. Both sons were fond of their stepfather, George, and devoted to their mother, Lillian, with whom they shared a distinct connection. George died in March 2018, and Lillian passed away in December of 2018; their deaths were a profound loss to Rodney and his family.

Rodney's loving wife, Lena, and their children are his paramount interests. Despite their professional demands, Rodney's and Lena's family is close-knit; they attend a myriad of sporting, school, cultural and other events and vacation with their five children annually. Rodney, Lena and children live in Bethesda, Maryland, where all the family enjoy their beautiful, commodious home.

Lillian Fannie Regina Waller Thomas Moore and Haywood O. Moore Family Pictures

Lillian and George, 1983

Newlyweds
May 29, 1979

Lillian and George

Lillian, a caring
nurse, mid-1980s

Rodney and Rob

Barbara, Rodney, Rob,
Mother and Lillian

Posing at the Pamunkey
Indian Reservation,
2000: Lillian, Rodney
and Hasani; Nataly and
her mother, Francia

Lillian, Mother's
Day, 1993

Lillian and Rodney

Rob and children,
Kweisi and Sequoia

Sequoia, Kweisi and
their mother, Tungi

Rodney and sons,
Hasani and Dakari

Dakari, Hasani and
their mother, Nataly

Ronald and his
niece, Noelle

Noelle and her mother,
Tanya Miller

Four of George's children: from left, Manuel, Lopez,
Conchita and Carmen; with George and Lillian

Aaliyah, Sequoia, Noelle;
second row: Lena and Lillian

Dakari and Hasani; second row: Rodney,
Kweisi, George and Manuel

Celebrating with Rodney and Lena. Seated: Manuel, Jewel,
Rob, Lillian, George; standing: Amaya, Aaliyah, Noelle,
Rodney, Robert Earl and Sallie Thomas, and Sequoia

Rob, stepping out

Rob in 2009

Rob, owner, CEO of Scrubnik Lawncare, Inc., 2013

Kweisi is part of "the few, the proud, the Marines," 2017

Sequoia, a beautiful young lady ready for graduation

Lillian and Kweisi at Parris Island, South Carolina, for his graduation, 2017

Rodney, Lillian and Rob, late 1980s

Rob, 1995

Rob and devoted friend, Patricia Finney, 2017

Rodney and Lena,
October 2012

The newlyweds, Rodney and Lena, with parents
and family: George and Lillian Moore, Rob Thomas,
Rodney and Lena, Sallie and Robert Thomas

Noelle Thomas
Honor Roll Student

"Little Miss"
Amaya Thomas

Aaliyah Foster
Honor Roll Student

Hasani and
Dakari Thomas

Hasani's son, Adrian
Miguel Thomas, 2018

Rodney, 2010

Betty Louise Waller Gray

Betty Waller Gray

Betty was born on April 21, 1946, in Richmond, fourth daughter of Richard and Florence Waller. Betty was a good student throughout her years in Richmond Public Schools. In 1963, she completed her high school education, graduating from Maggie L. Walker. She enrolled in Norfolk State College, majored in mathematics and received her bachelor's degree in mathematics in 1967. At Norfolk State, Betty was initiated into her beloved Alpha Kappa Alpha Sorority, Inc., in 1965. The sorority is very important to her and she joined the Upsilon Omega Chapter immediately following college graduation. She served as treasurer, Pan-Hellenic representative and chapter delegate for her first five national conventions. She continued her affiliation with AKA through the years, her motto being "AKA: Always Keep Active."

Soon after Betty's graduation from college, she began working for DuPont's Spruance Film Plant in Richmond. During the period 1967–1976, Betty, the sole female employee designated in the "exempt" category, often received written company memos with the request to wear a "shirt and tie" to meetings. What a strange request! Betty considers herself Richmond's "Hidden Figure." When DuPont transferred Betty to Orange, Texas, in 1976, she united with AKA Sorority's Epsilon Theta Omega Chapter and served as treasurer. While in Texas, Betty purchased her first home, in Port Arthur. Later, DuPont relocated her to Wilmington, Delaware, where Betty joined AKA's Zeta Omega Chapter.

Cynthia "Cindy" Johnson (Cummings), a friend from DuPont and later a student at VCU, was initiated into AKA as a general member. The two of them were instrumental in chartering VCU's Theta Rho Chapter of AKA in 1974. This was a grand accomplishment and occurred on Betty's birthday, April 21. Betty served as the chapter's first graduate advisor. Another Theta Rho soror was Forrestiner "Tina" Adams (Dickerson). Cindy and Tina remain Betty's best friends.

On July 8, 1978, Betty married Leonard Gray, a Richmond native. In June 1980, a prophet told Betty that she would receive a gift from God. That gift arrived on March 30, 1981, when Betty and Leonard became proud parents of daughter Leonetty Akeisha Gray.

Betty left her position with DuPont in 1982, returned to Richmond and was employed by Philip Morris. Soon thereafter, Betty and Leonard's marriage ended in divorce. Betty's priorities were caring for Leonetty and working. Her favorite hobby was bowling.

Travel was required while working at Philip Morris and Betty traveled often. One trip was to Minneapolis during the 1987 World Series. An ardent sports fan, Betty had "Super Box" seating at a Series game. In 1997, Betty purchased season tickets for the Richmond Rage (of the former American Basketball League, Women's Basketball League) and became self-appointed cheerleader (#1 Rage Fan). She appeared in *Vibe Magazine* and *The Style Weekly*, on ESPN and BET and in *The Richmond Times-Dispatch* and *Richmond Free Press* newspapers. Nike endorsed her and provided her with tennis shoes. Betty retired early from Philip Morris in June 1998. In 2001, she was interviewed and pictured in *Money* magazine's article "Retire Your Way."

Betty, a mathematics and computer software expert, used her extensive computer skills when, in 1987, she established BG Express Personalized Computer Service. She created banners, flyers, business cards, tickets and more. For five years, she issued a family newsletter, *Waller We-View*. She has also used her skills in support of the sorority in the roles of finance committee member, treasurer and previous technology chairman.

Betty's interests and hobbies include participating in civil rights and women's rights marches and activities; and she is a travel, football, women's basketball and bowling enthusiast. She played a significant role in establishing the Norfolk State University's Richmond Alumni Chapter, which was chartered June 8, 1970, as documented in *Upward: A History of Norfolk State University*, by Dr. Lyman Beecher Brooks. Betty became the chapter's first president. Also, Betty has volunteered with the Multiple Sclerosis Society and the NAACP. She served as a volunteer mentor in the Richmond Public Schools and helped establish a Teen Center in her Chesterfield County neighborhood.

A lifelong member of Moore Street Baptist Church, Betty sings with the Joy of Jubal Choir and is a member of the finance committee along with other ministries. In her work with the finance committee, she uses her knowledge of technology to assist the group. A fellow church member stated, "Everyone knows that Betty is the go-to person if you have a computer problem."

In recent years, Betty has worked in various positions, including adjunct instructor at Virginia Union University; math substitute and tutor in Richmond Public Schools; and trainer, sales representative and computer analyst with major firms. Currently, Betty is a sales team member, computer administrator and website manager at Waller & Company, the family jewelry business.

Betty and Leonetty take mother-daughter trips each year. On one trip, they traveled cross-country by train. Highlights were visits to Las Vegas, Los Angeles and Albuquerque (where they rode in a hot-air balloon). Other destinations were Cuba, Niagara Falls, Coral Springs, Florida; and Birmingham, Selma and Montgomery, Alabama. Their trip to Europe included visits to Paris and London. They attended several Colts preseason football games in New York and in Indianapolis. Additional trips were to Muhammad Ali's childhood home, gravesite and museum in Lexington, Kentucky; and many times to the Spirit Trade Show featuring Greek paraphernalia.

In addition, Betty and Leonetty worked the polls in Chesterfield County in support of Democrats and as proud advocates of President Obama's campaign. He was elected the 44th President of the United States in 2008, the first African American to hold this prestigious office. Betty and Leonetty attended both Obama inaugurations in Washington. In 1990, they were pleased to attend the inauguration of Governor L. Douglas Wilder in Richmond, Virginia's first Black governor.

Betty participated in the 1963 March on Washington, and she marched with daughter Leonetty for the 30th and 50th anniversaries of the historic march. During the 2013 march, Betty carried a sign indicating that she had joined in all three marches. She was photographed holding her sign and the photo was featured in the *Wall Street Journal, Ebony, Essence* and in other publications throughout the world. Richmond's NBC12 (WWBT) broadcast an interview about her civil rights experiences. "I can't really grasp what she had to live through," Leonetty Gray said of her mother's life.

Betty states, "As the daughter of such a phenomenal woman as Mother, I continue the legacy she began as a dedicated and influential woman."

Leonetty Akeisha Gray

Leonetty Gray

Leonetty was born on March 30, 1981, in Wilmington, Delaware; the only child of Leonard A. and Betty Waller Gray. Leonetty grew up in Richmond and attended Richmond Public Schools. She enrolled in Norfolk State University and earned a bachelor's degree in mass communications (with honors) in 2003. She received a master's degree in educational studies (also with honors) in 2014 from the University of Phoenix.

Since 2007, she has taught in Richmond Public Schools. Currently, Leonetty teaches language arts at Henderson Middle School, where she is positively impacting hundreds of young people and mentors current and former students, some of whom have completed college.

Leonetty has a lifelong interest in reading as a result of being read to by her babysitter. Even in the early grades, she received awards for reading an exceptional number of books. As a young girl, Leonetty was enamored by Maya Angelou's poem "Phenomenal Woman," which she recited on myriad occasions. Cooking, trying new recipes and entertaining family and friends are among Leonetty's pastimes, along with annual mother-daughter trips to various locales in the U.S. and abroad. She relishes interacting with senior citizens; in the past, Leonetty had close nurturing relationships with both her Grandmother Waller and Grandmother Winston, who are now deceased.

Since her baptism at Moore Street Church on Christmas Day, 1988, Leonetty has been an active member, participating in Sunday School and youth activities, volunteering with Vacation Bible School and other church functions. She also enhances the church's ministries through teaching Zumba and assisting with cell phone apps.

Leonetty is a member of Alpha Kappa Alpha Sorority, Inc., and was initiated in Theta Omega Omega Chapter in Montgomery County, Maryland, in 2006. She is now an active member of Upsilon Omega Chapter in Richmond and serves on the AKA Graduate

Advisors Council for undergraduate chapters at Virginia Commonwealth University, Virginia Union University and the University of Richmond.

She has been recognized as an "exemplary teacher" by the Richmond Public School System and was accepted to the Teachers in the Movement at the University of Virginia. Also, Leonetty was selected as clinical resident coach in the Richmond Residency Program and was nominated to pursue the National Teacher Board Certification.

At just 10 years old, Leonetty was asked to look after her Grandmother Waller and Leonetty says, "That began the nurturer by nature lifestyle I have led for 25-plus years." Leonetty is a devoted daughter; she and her mother, Betty, have a special bond and relish their time together.

Our Twins! They are Beautiful

Barbara and Betty's photograph at the Formal Ball of the Army Reserve Officer's Training Corps program at Norfolk State University, 1964

A wonderful day! Barbara, Mother and Betty at the twins' graduation from Norfolk State, 1967

Betty Louise Waller Gray and Leonetty Gray Family Photos

Betty is ready for her
Senior Prom, June 1963

Betty's Maggie L. Walker
High cheerleading
letter, 1963

A proud AKA, Betty is
wearing her sorority
pin and guard.

At Norfolk State's
Homecoming, 1974

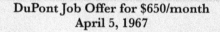

DU PONT

E. I. DU PONT DE NEMOURS & COMPANY
RICHMOND, VIRGINIA 23212   Richmond, Virginia
April 5, 1967

Miss Betty L. Waller

Dear Miss Waller:

We enjoyed your visit to our plant and I am pleased to
offer you a position in our Systems Development Section at a starting salary of $ 650.00 per month.

Traveling expenses to your initial assignment will be
paid by Du Pont.

We hope you will decide to come with us and look forward
to your reply.

Supervisor - Employee Relations

DuPont Job Offer for $650/month
April 5, 1967

Betty's first home at
3221 Thomas Blvd.,
Port Arthur, Texas

Wedding Day,
June 8, 1978

Leonetty at three
months old, 1981

Leonetty at age four, 1985

Betty and Leonetty, 1986

Leonetty, Betty and Lillian are using
a hand pump to obtain water.

Robin, Leonetty and their
mothers at daughters' Beulah
Elementary Graduation, 1991

Grandmother Waller
(Nini) and Leonetty, 1992

Leonetty and
Grandmother Winston
(Grandma), 2006

Leonetty, a high
school senior, 1999

Leonetty and parents,
Betty and Leonard, 1999

Leonetty, October 2003

Betty, *Money* magazine
photo, 2001

It was a frigid day! Betty and
Leonetty at President Obama's
Inauguration, January 20, 2009

50th Anniversary of the
March on Washington,
August 28, 2013

AKA Legislative Day at Virginia
State Capitol; Tracey, Betty, Leonetty
and Deanna, February 17, 2014

Betty's Golden Soror
50-Year AKA celebration,
Atlanta Boule, 2016

**Betty at 50th Maggie L.
Walker High Class of 1963
Reunion, October 2013**

**50th Norfolk State
University Graduation
Reunion Medallion, 2017**

**Betty's 70th birthday
party had a 1970s
theme, 2016**

Leonetty swims with dolphins, 2010

**Leonetty, while in Cuba, stands
beside a classic vehicle, 2017**

**Mother and daughter
at Niagara Falls, 2014**

**Riding in a hot-air balloon in
Albuquerque, New Mexico, 2014**

Barbara Florence Waller Nealy

Barbara Waller Nealy

Barbara was born April 21, 1946, in Richmond, the fifth daughter of Richard and Florence Waller. Barbara completed Richmond Public Schools and graduated from Maggie L. Walker High in 1963. She then enrolled at Norfolk State University and received a bachelor's degree in English (with honors) in 1967. At Norfolk State, Barbara was initiated into Delta Sigma Theta Sorority Inc., Epsilon Theta Chapter in 1965. Later, Barbara earned a master's degree in adult education with a concentration in gerontology from Coppin State University, Baltimore in 1985, with a 4.0 GPA.

After completing her undergraduate degree, Barbara began her teaching career at Armstrong High School in Richmond, where she taught English. While vacationing in Florida during Christmas break in 1968, she met Robert Lee Nealy, a Florida native. They were wed on Memorial Day in 1969 and moved to Edgewood, Maryland, his military posting. To this union, two girls were born: Ta-Tanisha LaFlorence, on February 3, 1971, in Edgewood; and Ta-Tianna Kamaria on September 9, 1979, in Baltimore.

In 1971, Barbara and her expanding family moved to Annapolis and she taught English at Annapolis Senior High. Later, Barbara served as a community parent worker with the Anne Arundel County Head Start Agency. She was promoted to planning research and evaluation officer for the AAC Community Action Agency. Subsequently, the family relocated to Baltimore County, where Barbara was employed as a planning analyst by the Baltimore County Office of Aging. Following her time in Annapolis, she also taught high school English, French and speech and drama at public schools in Harford County, Maryland, and in Baltimore.

Barbara was a devoted mother to her girls and exposed each of them to many positive activities and events. She ensured that they were well behaved and refined in their demeanor. She inspired their educational achievements.

Upon completing her master's degree, Barbara worked at Woodstock Job Corps as a teacher for GED preparation. Subsequent to that employment, she taught English in the

Baltimore City Public Schools for two years. In the mid-1990s, she worked in retail and again taught GED preparation part-time.

She also became a cosmetic consultant for Fashion 220 and worked with this company for 20 years. She initiated her own innovative Nail Care with Foot Fun Program, which was featured in the national *Fashion 220* publication. Barbara did makeovers of friends and customers at home shows. This was the perfect vocation for her; she was a "fashionista." Barbara always looked her best and was beautifully attired for every occasion. She was a thrifty and thoughtful shopper. Barbara used these skills to assist customers when she worked in retail and also as a consumer.

She relocated to Richmond in 1998 and shortly thereafter, her marriage ended in divorce. There, Barbara again became a congregant at Moore Street, her home church, where she was baptized in 1955; worked at Waller & Company Jewelers; and renewed her membership with Delta Sigma Theta. After retirement, she moved to a senior apartment complex, where she met Charles Simmons. They later became dear friends and enjoyed concerts, evenings out and other activities together until his health deteriorated and he passed away in 2010.

Barbara had a number of special interests, including facilitating annual presentations on Black history, a lifelong passion. Also, she presented seminars that addressed breast cancer awareness. Barbara's outgoing personality enabled her to make numerous friends easily wherever she resided. Exceptionally thoughtful and generous, for many years, Barbara ministered to family, friends and church members with greeting cards that inspired and encouraged them.

Barbara was suffering from a lingering illness, and as a result, relocated to a facility in Virginia Beach, Virginia, where she was close to her daughter Ta-Tanisha, son-in-law, Frank, and her grandchildren, Autumn Joy and Joseph Robert. Barbara was a doting grandmother and enjoyed spending holidays with her daughters and family. All were devoted to Barbara.

In March 2020, Barbara and all the family witnessed the wedding of daughter Ta-Tianna in Charlotte, North Carolina, via an electronic connection and welcomed Chris McFadden to the family.

Our treasured sister, Barbara, passed away on May 1, 2020. She was funeralized on May 13, 2020, by her pastor, the Reverend Dr. Alonza Lawrence, and is inurned at Forest

Lawn Cemetery in Richmond. Her service was viewed electronically by family and friends who were unable to attend due to the COVID-19 pandemic. Barbara is beloved and is greatly missed by all.

Ta-Tanisha Nealy Walton

Ta-Tanisha "Nisha" LaFlorence Nealy Walton

Ta-Tanisha was born on February 3, 1971, in Edgewood, Maryland, firstborn of Robert and Barbara Waller Nealy.

A good student throughout her academic years, she was enrolled in honors classes in high school. Ta-Tanisha completed her elementary and secondary education in Baltimore Public Schools. Nisha was a physical education leader and drum major, and she received a band scholarship to attend Norfolk State University. In college, she played clarinet in NSU's Spartan Legion Band and oboe in NSU's Spartan Legion Orchestra. Ta-Tanisha was also an NSU Band Hot Ice dancer. In 1992, she was initiated in Delta Sigma Theta Sorority, Inc., Epsilon Theta Chapter. She received her bachelor's degree in English (early childhood education) with honors in 1993 and a master's degree in urban education (administrative) in 1999, also from NSU.

Ta-Tanisha has been employed by the Norfolk Public School System since graduating and has held various positions of increasing responsibility, including literacy teacher, instructional specialist, early childhood teacher specialist, kindergarten coordinator and assessment coordinator. Ta-Tanisha is the recipient of several honors: Teacher of the Year, Apple for the Teacher and School Bell awards.

She married Joseph Francis Walton in 2001. Frank, a native of Virginia Beach, is a funeral service director and college professor, and has served as president of the Virginia State Board of Funeral Directors and Embalmers.

Longtime residents of Virginia Beach, Frank and Nisha are the proud parents of two children: daughter Autumn Joy, born August 19, 2003; and son Joseph Robert, born October 17, 2008. In 2019, Autumn was excited to obtain her Virginia state driver's license and drives her grandmother Barbara's vehicle. She has worked part-time as a birthday party host and coach at the Virginia Beach Field House. Autumn plans to attend a Historically Black College and University after graduation. She is now a high school senior at Landstown High. An honor roll student, Autumn was a mentor to the ninth graders and participated in the Girls Who Code Club. She has volunteered with Upward basketball and served as an assistant coach for the fifth- to sixth-grade team. During the summer of 2020, Autumn was employed as a lifeguard.

Joseph is a sixth grader at Landstown Middle; the subjects he likes most are science and physical education. He is curious about nature and enjoys reading about animals. He conducts science experiments with household items, listens to music, plays basketball and baseball, goes to the beach and plays video games. Joe has received certificates for out-standing behavior and good character.

The family is keen on attending church and sporting events, entertaining family and friends, visiting the library, participating in cultural events and taking vacations. As a youth, Nisha was very active in Epworth Methodist Church in Baltimore. She, Frank and family have membership at Bute Street Baptist Church in Norfolk.

Ta-Tianna Kamaria Nealy McFadden

Ta-Tianna Nealy McFadden

Ta-Tianna was born on September 9, 1979, in Baltimore, second daughter of Robert and Barbara Waller Nealy. Ta-Tianna completed her elementary and secondary education in Baltimore Public Schools. In 2003, she received a bachelor's degree in information systems, with honors, from Norfolk State University. While a student, she played the cymbals in NSU's Marching Spartan Legion Band and was initiated into Zeta Phi Beta Sorority, Inc. Ta-Tianna was awarded a Master of Business Administration degree from Southeastern University in Washington, DC, in 2008. She is a certified project management professional and risk management professional.

She delivers medium- to large-scale information technology projects with full responsibility and accountability for the outcomes. She has been in the field of IT for over 14 years with an emphasis on project management, database administration and business analysis.

In her career, Ta-Tianna has held various leadership roles in the private and public sectors and has worked at Fortune 50 companies including Wells-Fargo and Lowe's. Booz Allen Hamilton is among the Fortune 100 companies where she has held significant positions.

She joined the Washington Chapter of the National Black MBA Association, (NBMBAA), and served in several roles: acting membership chair, acting corporate development lead and student outreach chair. After relocating to Charlotte, North Carolina, Ta-Tianna joined the NBMBAA Charlotte Chapter and has been director of scholarships and the lead in corporate development.

Ta-Tianna is the recipient of several honors and awards, including the following: MBA of the Year, 2013, and President's Award, 2012, from the NBMBAA Washington Chapter; Zeta of the Year Award, 2016, given by Zeta Phi Beta, Psi Mu Zeta Chapter; and the very prestigious Women of Color STEM Rising Star Award, 2013.

Her hobbies and interests include cooking seafood, attending concerts and festivals and traveling, nationally and internationally. She is very proud of her "small debut" role in the movie *Stomp the Yard*. Along with her work-related activities, Ta-Tianna is very engaged in her community. She is passionate about the community and creating value.

On March 25, 2020, Ta-Tianna was married to Chris McFadden, a native of Rock Hill, South Carolina. Due to the horrific COVID-19 pandemic experienced worldwide, the newlyweds' plans for a church wedding on March 29 in Charlotte, with attendance by many family and friends, were canceled. Instead, the couple exchanged their vows in a small and meaningful ceremony witnessed by family and friends via videoconference. Ta-Tianna has developed a tender attachment and deep love for her stepdaughter, Madyson, who was pictured with her dad, Chris, and Ta-Tianna on their wedding invitation. All the family wish the couple a wonderful life together and many blessings.

Barbara Waller Nealy, Ta-Tanisha Nealy Walton and Ta-Tianna Nealy McFadden Family Photos

Barbara dressed for her Senior Prom, 1963

Barbara's Maggie L. Walker High School cheerleading letter, 1963

Barbara, mid-1960s

Ta-Tanisha and Barbara, early 1970s

Ta-Tanisha at age four, 1974

Ta-Tianna at age three, 1984

Barbara's display at Jewel's home for a Finelle Cosmetic Show

Barbara and Betty, about 2000

Barbara, Ta-Tianna and Ta-Tanisha

Barbara, 1993 in Norfolk

Barbara, in center, surrounded by grandchildren Autumn and Joseph; and daughters Ta-Tanisha and Ta-Tianna

Barbara at Christmas

Barbara and her devoted friend, Charles Simmons, mid-2000s

Nisha's
high school
graduation
photo, 1989

Nisha and parents
Barbara and Robert at her
graduation party, 1989

Nisha graduates
from Norfolk
State, 1993

Ta-Tanisha and
Frank Walton's
wedding day,
June 2001; from
the left: Robert
Nealy, Barbara
Nealy, Nisha,
Frank, June and
Joseph Walton

Nisha and Frank

Nisha and Frank's
daughter, Autumn,
is a beautiful teen.

Joseph, their son,
enjoys basketball.

Joseph, Frank, Nisha
and Autumn have
fun at the shore.

Ta-Tianna, a poised
and lovely teen

Joseph, Nisha, Barbara,
Ta-Tianna and Autumn

Chris McFadden and
Ta-Tianna, 2019

Chris, Ta-Tianna and Madyson

Chris and Ta-Tianna's
photo from their wedding
invitation, March 2020

Newlyweds Chris and
Ta-Tianna McFadden
celebrate on their wedding
day, March 25, 2020

Memorable Times Together

Aubrey, Joyce, Jean and LeRoy vacation at a Poconos, Pennsylvania, resort, 1986.

Mother and Lill relax in Freeport, The Bahamas, 1987.

Betty and Jewel on a Caribbean cruise from San Juan, Puerto Rico, 1993

Having fun on the Bermuda cruise, 2006; Joyce, Lillian and Betty

Betty and Lillian looking glamorous on the cruise to Bermuda

Barbara, Joyce, Lill and Charles Simmons take in the beautiful scenery on the cruise.

How exciting! We are embarking for Bermuda: Lillian, Leonetty, Betty, Barbara, Joyce, LeCount and Jewel, 2006.

Waller sisters at Dungee Reunion; Jewel, Joyce, Lillian, Betty and Barbara, 1998, Raleigh, North Carolina

Dungee Family Reunion. Standing: Leonetty and Ta-Tianna; seated: Jewel, Lillian, Jean, Richard, Betty, Barbara and Joyce, 2003, Falls Church, Virginia

Dungee Family Reunion, 2009, hosted by the Waller Family; held in Greenbelt, Maryland, and Washington, DC. Sallie and Robert Thomas Sr., Leonetty Gray, Rodney Thomas, Tanya Miller, LeCount, Jewel, Richard, Manuel Moore, Lillian, Jean, George, Joyce, Betty, Robert Thomas Jr. and Tungi (Valerie) Thomas; Lillian's grandchildren, left to right: Noelle, Dakari, Hasani, Kweisi and Sequoia Thomas

We cruised to Bermuda in 2006
with Maggie Walker High's
50 Year Grads!
Richard,
Leonetty, Joyce, Lillian and Betty;
Charles and LeCount;
Jean, Barbara and Jewel.

A memorable trip! Our family cruised
to Alaska in 2008: Aubrey, Jewel,
Richard, Joyce, LeCount and Jean.

We had a splendid time at Baltimore's
Inner Harbor in the
mid-1980s; Barbara, Lillian and Betty.

Actor Bernie Casey, the
featured guest at the 2008
Dungee Family Reunion in
Los Angeles is surrounded
by Jean, Lillian and Jewel.

Leonetty, Betty and Lillian
are all smiles as they begin
our family trip to Alaska
aboard the *Celebrity
Infinity* cruise ship.

Part Seven

Following Their Lead

Chapter 17

Waller & Company Today and Our Entrepreneurial Legacy Through Three Generations

Richard, 1968

The story of our family's jewelry business continues to shine as brightly as the gold, silver and diamonds displayed in the beautiful and well-appointed store located at 19 East Broad Street in downtown Richmond and online at www.wallerjewelry.com. The owner, our brother Richard Jr., started work in the company as a young child, just as our grandfather had begun repairing clocks as a youngster before opening a jewelry store, M. C. Waller Jewelry, in 1900.

Richard's early beginnings in watch repairing originated when he was in elementary school. In most families of our day, the older children worked, and ours was no exception. Afternoons on school days and on Saturdays during the late 1940s and early to mid-1950s, Richard and Jewel worked with Daddy and our uncles in the jewelry store.

Every day at work, the siblings waited on clients, wiped the glass showcase, cleaned and polished jewelry and ran errands to pick up supplies and parts. Richard's primary task was winding watches that had been repaired. At that time, watches had mechanical parts and this function needed to be performed every day. These timepieces were very popular until about 1978, when most watches produced were battery-operated. Richard frequently

In 1970, Waller & Company Jewelers moved to 105 East Broad Street., a major milestone for an African American family-owned business.

Continuing the legacy. In 1968, Richard opened his first store, which operated at 405 North First Street.

visited a nearby pharmacy to retrieve cigar boxes that were used to store the watches as they were in various stages of repair.

Jewel's favorite assignment was helping shoppers. She relished showing and selling the beautiful jewelry items that lined the showcase. With the rudimentary skills of a 12- or 13-year-old, Jewel was the company bookkeeper, writing checks and recording suppliers' invoices and payments on wide sheets of columnar paper and adding the figures to arrive at the totals. These duties stimulated her desire later on to work in the college's finance office while earning her degree in business.

Since the store was adjacent to Grandpa Waller's residence, Richard and Jewel visited Grandpa almost daily. Grandpa also came down to the store to sit and participate in some of the chatter about the watches and jewelry that patrons had left for service, but he was ailing and no longer working as a jeweler. Richard enjoyed eating snacks and meals with Grandpa, and Richard's favorites were the delicious vegetable soup and gingerbread Grandpa prepared. Living two doors from the jewelry shop were Uncle Tom, Aunt Marie and Jean. At times, while "on the job" as a youngster, Richard visited them and helped himself to their candy while viewing *Howdy Doody* on their television, a special treat since we didn't have a television in our place.

Jewel spent even more time with Grandpa Waller, as she was the person designated to serve his dinner each day after school. She valued this one-on-one time with Grandpa and believes he inspired her interest in business and helped create her entrepreneurial spirit. Jewel felt special when visiting Grandpa and was thrilled when he urged her to eat as much as she wanted of the delicious apple pie, lamb and other good food that had been prepared for him. She did not have to share with siblings.

During Richard's and Jewel's daily visits, Grandpa asked about their schoolwork, subjects they were studying and progress they were making. He gave them advice that would be necessary for success in any retail establishment. Arriving to the store early and opening on time, working hard, treating customers with respect and dignity and keeping your word were among the life lessons he imparted. Grandpa was always encouraging and stated that he was pleased with them and expressed appreciation for their work in the store. Listening to him, Richard and Jewel grasped the fact that Grandpa started a venture some 50 years earlier and accomplished so much. He became a successful entrepreneur despite the obstacles he faced and so could they!

Not only did Richard and Jewel earn spending money working, but they learned self-discipline and the commitment to complete any assigned tasks. They gained experience and skills they would apply throughout their lives.

Richard did not understand that during these early years working in the store, he was being groomed to someday take over this enterprise. When he finished high school in 1956, Richard followed in the footsteps of Grandpa Waller, Daddy and two uncles, and worked full time. Daddy had started teaching Richard the skills of watch repairing and his preparation continued under the tutelage of our uncles Junius and Thomas, as he worked beside them for several years.

Over time and with extensive on-the-job training and the completion of technical courses, Richard became a Master Jeweler and Watchmaker. He opened his first jewelry store, Waller & Company Jewelers, in 1968 on First Street in Richmond's downtown. To better serve a growing clientele, Richard's store moved to Broad Street in 1970, representing a major achievement for a small African American family-owned firm. At that time, few minority-owned operations were located in the city's downtown shopping district.

A few years later, the Leigh Street shop closed. Richard consolidated M. C. Waller & Sons and Waller & Company Jewelers. In 1980, Waller & Company relocated to 19 East Broad Street, where it remains.

Richard has experienced numerous challenges and opportunities as he has effectively operated the company for over five decades. Richard says, "I strive to always put God first." Further, he has said, "It is by God's grace that this business has survived and that the family's business legacy fills me with pride and inspires me."

In January 1987, Waller & Company's present location almost went up in flames when the department store located adjacent to it experienced a major fire and was destroyed. The store suffered extensive water damage, but we were grateful that the building was spared from the fire. Although Richard was disheartened at the time, he vowed to stand strong. Fewer retail establishments in the downtown district, and many structural changes implemented by the city, have negatively impacted Waller & Company's growth, including parking restrictions and revised bus transit schedules. Nevertheless, hard work, determination and faith, that of a mustard seed, have sustained him over these years.

Now as we complete the writing of this chronicle in the fall of 2020, our family business is hoping to withstand the extraordinary obstacles brought on by the recent COVID-19 pandemic. The vast extent of its accompanying deleterious effect has very severely impacted families, communities and businesses. We pray that God's grace and mercy will sustain us all as we endure this.

Richard's sons, Richard III (Rick) and David, joined their dad in this line of work. Rick entered the firm in 1987 and David in 1997. What Richard Jr. had learned, he taught his sons. They gained the ability necessary to build customer relationships and trust as well as the skills to repair jewelry and to employ effective sales techniques. Rick and David acquired the knowledge to quickly discern customers' possible preferences, and to select and sell to these clients the jewelry they fancied most. All of these proficiencies continue to sustain the company today.

Waller & Company has furnished an extensive selection of beautiful jewelry and repaired thousands of watches and jewelry items through the years. Dedicated customers who have bought their watches and wedding rings from the business, return to buy that special gift for their spouse's anniversary and birthday. Others come for unique crosses for baptism, pendants for graduation, watches for the newly initiated sorority member or for a custom-designed item. Some patrons are accompanied by their parents or grandparents who have also been longtime clients. Various satisfied shoppers have stated that they wouldn't purchase jewelry anywhere else.

Over the years, the company has had an incredibly dedicated staff of employees and relatives who aim to provide excellent service. Among the longtime loyal employees were Mrs. Ethel Jefferson and her son, Wayne. Our father had taught a young man the jewelry-repairing skills years ago and Richard taught Wayne, who used these competencies to operate his own establishment. Mr. Melvin Hill, a watchmaker, and Mr. Everett Washington were also employees for many years. Mr. Tyrone Gresham, Richard's high school classmate, whose previous career was with the federal government, was another dependable employee. Richard III's wife, Kim, has been an integral part of the company since 2002. Our sister Betty has worked with the firm and the field staff for many years, and our sister Barbara was employed at the store for a short while. On occasion, Jean, Richard Jr.'s wife, and their grandson, Alex, assist in the business.

In 1997, Jewel returned to work in the enterprise, working remotely from Maryland after retiring from her career in the federal government. In rejoining the firm, Jewel's goals were to expand the company's client base and gain more market share for Waller & Company. She obtained a Maryland state sales license and established the field service division, which operated beyond the physical confines of the store. To promote this new component, she engaged professionals to develop a website for jewelry purchases by online customers. Sister Joyce is an essential part of the field service staff, as was our sister Lillian. Nieces Leonetty and Ta-Tianna have participated in sales activities. Our sister Betty utilizes her extensive computer expertise to manage online concerns, including promotions and sales for the company's online customers, fulfillment of online orders and ancillary website issues. In addition, she has responsibility for in-store computer operations.

From 2003 to 2007, the company operated a satellite store and a kiosk in Virginia Center Commons Mall in Glen Allen. At this location, the firm gained additional shoppers and met the jewelry service needs of those in the Northside section of the Richmond area. After closing this site, a number of these clients have remained steadfast patrons of Waller & Company at the Broad Street location.

Like our Grandpa Waller and Daddy, Richard Jr. is well respected in the community. He has received many honors and awards for his integrity and dedication and the company's longevity. These include acknowledgment by Zeta Phi Beta Sorority for Outstanding Accomplishments in Economic Development, 1977; Award of Excellence for Support and Service to People of Our Community, from United Way of Greater Richmond, 1989; the Metropolitan Business League Economic Growth and Development Award, 1996; and the Astoria Beneficial Club 1997 Corporate Award.

A distinguished tribute was the Metropolitan Business League's Lifetime Achievement Award, 2004, which was presented in recognition of Waller & Company's 103 years of continuous service to the Richmond community. Part of this recognition was an MBL scholarship to attend an intensive program for minority business owners at Dartmouth College in New Hampshire. This rewarding experience at such a prestigious institution afforded Richard the opportunity to fine-tune his managerial and business skills in response to our country's changing economy.

Richard was further recognized with the Ralph Samuels Business Award for Outstanding Development of Black Entrepreneurship and Economic Awareness in the Local Community, 2011; selected as First Place Winner of the MBL's 2019 Small Business Grant; and was nominated by the Richmond Retail Merchants Association as Business Person of the Year, 2019.

Waller & Company was featured in *Richmond Magazine's* January 5, 2020, edition in the article "A Lasting Legacy: Jackson Ward's Waller & Company Jewelers Celebrates 120 Years in Business." In March 2020, the City of Richmond acknowledged the firm with a trophy that reads as follows:

Minority Business of the Year

Waller and Company Jewelers, LLC

Richard A. Waller Jr.

Under Richard's leadership, the store has continued to grow, prosper and remain successful. The business is well known throughout the region and enjoys a fine reputation for quality sales and service. It is highly ranked among Richmond's jewelers and is recognized by Jewelers of America, Inc., Southern Jewelers, the Better Business Bureau, the Chronometer Club and Tri-Cities Watchmakers Guild, where Richard was past president. In 2017, Waller & Company was acknowledged by the *Prime Buyer's Report* as one of the best jewelry stores in the Richmond area, having met requirements for value and honesty. Richard Jr. has affiliated with local and national business organizations, such as Downtown Richmond, Inc., now Venture Richmond, where he has served on various committees and represented the interests of small downtown businesses.

Waller & Company has continued to experience some vestiges of racism. For several years in the mid-1990s to the early 2000s, Richard, his wife Jean, and other store-affiliated relatives attended the Jeweler's Circular Keystone International Jewelry Show. At this annual trade show for store owners and buyers, wholesalers from around the world display an extensive array of jewelry. The Wallers were always astounded at the stares received from other participants and were surprised when some exhibitors singled out our family members to closely examine their credentials. Consistent with their resilient spirit, they always rose above this animus and proceeded to select beautiful jewelry for the store, just as other owners and buyers were there to do.

Beginning in 2015, Richard Jr. semi-retired, and now works part-time. Richard III is store manager and jewelry repairman, while David is assistant manager and marketing director. Richard Jr. and his sons have continued to build on the company's foundation of excellence, honesty and proficiency. They have incorporated technological advances and innovations, including the internet and social networks, to advance the company's presence far beyond its physical locale.

The Waller owners and staff are committed to carrying out the tradition of providing superior service and exquisite jewelry to satisfy the most selective shopper. Other services include gem remounting, engraving, ring sizing and jewelry repair. The business sells paraphernalia for sororities, fraternities, and the Eastern Star and Masonic organizations. Waller & Company pledges to continue its custom of community service by collaborating and participating with local and regional community events.

In April 1990, owners, staff and supporters proudly celebrated the company's 90th Anniversary with a reception and sale. In 2000, its centennial year, Waller & Company was honored with a City of Richmond Proclamation from Timothy M. Kaine, Mayor. The tribute reads in part:

> To recognize the shining achievement and the noble legacy reflected in the
> 100th Anniversary of Waller and Company Jewelers.

At this time in 2020, we commemorate the founding of this business by our grandfather and great-grandfather, Marcellus Carrington Waller Sr., 120 years ago in 1900. We Wallers firmly believe that Waller & Company remains the oldest continuously operated African American family-owned jewelry retail and repair operation in all of these United States! We are extremely grateful for this achievement and are proud of the firm's rich 120-year history. We look forward to serving our valued customers who have patronized the store through the years, and new Richmond area, regional and national clientele.

We believe that the manner in which we treat customers and employees is a central reason for the company's longevity. Community activism and spiritual values play a key role as well. We give God all praise and glory for sustaining us and the company. Each receipt has printed on it the words "John 3:16," which allude to our brother Richard's favorite scripture, "For God so loved the world that He gave his only begotten son that whosoever believes in Him shall not perish, but have everlasting life."

Highlights of Waller & Company

Carla Waller, Richard III
and Mother assemble
a case of jewelry for
display at an exhibit.

Richard, Jean, David and Richard III

Mr. Hill, experienced
watchmaker employed
by Waller & Company,
and Uncle Tom

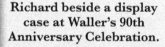

Jean and her friend Irene
Morgan at the Waller & Co.'s
90th Anniversary Celebration

Richard beside a display
case at Waller's 90th
Anniversary Celebration.

Uncle Tom, Cousin Jean,
Aunt Marie, Mother and
Aunt Geneva celebrate.

At the celebration, from left to right: Jewel, Cousin
Jean, Elsie, Leonetty, Betty, Lillian, Joyce and Jean, 1990

Anniversary Celebration and
Reception: Uncle Tom, Cousin
Jean and Lillian, 1990

Anniversary Reception: Richard
III, Betty and Richard Jr.

The City of Richmond
presented this
Proclamation to Waller &
Company on the occasion
of its 100th year.

A Waller brochure, with
Grandfather Waller on the
cover

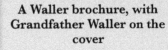

A custom display plate
to celebrate Waller &
Co.'s centennial year

Waller & Co. Family in white, vending at Plymouth Congregational UCC, Washington, DC. Left to right: Lillian, Jewel, Betty, Joyce and Mrs. Cooper, church member and show coordinator, 1997

Jewel at a Waller show at Aubrey and Joyce's home

A Waller & Co. Jewelry show at Joyce's home; Lillian, Jewel and Richard

A Waller Family vending event. Seated: Betty; left to right: Lillian, Barbara, Elsie, Jean, Jewel and Joyce

Richard III, Richard Jr. and Alex

Owners Richard Waller Jr., center, his sons Richard III on his right and David on his left

Continuing the Tradition

Since 1980, Waller & Company has served customers at 19 East Broad Street, Richmond

Current Business Card www.wallerjewelry.com

Alex, jeweler-in-training, 1990s

David Waller, 2020 (Photo by Jay Paul)

Richard is wearing an eye loupe as he repairs a watch.

The Waller staff stands ready to serve their loyal customers: Richard III, Kim, Tyrone Gresham, Betty, Richard Jr. and David, 2020 (Photo by Jay Paul)

Photo courtesy of March Funeral Home

Two views of the Waller Mural painted
on one side of the Waller store

2020 Best of Richmond
Award, Jewelers Category

Our Entrepreneurial Legacy Through Three Generations

	The FIRST Generation	
	Marcellus Carrington Waller Sr. M. C. Waller & Sons Jewelers Illustrious Entrepreneur- Founder, Owner, Innovator 1873-1957	
	Legacy Generation 1	
*Marcellus "Junius" Carrington Waller Jr. Master Jeweler and Watch Repairman M. C. Waller & Sons Jewelers Co-Owner/Manager	***Richard Alexander Waller Sr.** Master Jeweler and Watch Repairman M. C. Waller & Sons Jewelers Co-Owner/Manager	***Thomas Antonio Waller** Master Jeweler and Watch Repairman M. C. Waller & Sons Jewelers Co-Owner/Manager
	Legacy Generation 2	
Richard Alexander Waller Jr. Jeweler and Watchmaker Waller & Company Jewelers Owner/Manager 1973-Current	**Jean Jones Waller** Waller & Company Jewelers Store Sales and Support Staff Wife of Richard A. Waller Jr.	**Betty Waller Gray** Waller & Company Jewelers Store and Field Sales Staff Computer Technical Support, Website Sales, Promotions, Etc. B. G. Express Computer Services
Jewel Waller Davis Waller & Company Jewelers Field Sales Staff Developer/ Manager, Website Development Coordinator	**Joyce Waller Baden** Waller & Company Jewelers Field Sales Staff Online Sales Promotions All That and More Gifts	***Lillian Waller Moore** Waller & Company Jewelers Field Sales Staff Hali's Enterprises Founder/ Owner
*Barbara Waller Nealy Waller & Company Jewelers Store Sales Staff Lady Finelle Cosmetics Sales Agent and Consultant		**LeCount R. Davis Sr.** Certified Financial Planner Trailblazer Financial Management Consultant Founder/Owner
	Legacy Generation 3	
Richard Alexander Waller III Waller & Company Jewelers Jeweler and Watch Repairman Co-Owner/Manager	**Kim Lacy Waller** Waller & Company Jewelers Sales, Repairs and Management Assistance Wife of Richard A. Waller III	**David M. Waller, Esq.** Waller & Company Jewelers Jeweler and Watch Repairman, Advertising Manager Co-Owner/Co-Manager Contract Attorney
Robert E. Thomas Jr. SCRUBNIK Landscape Company Hyattsville, MD Founder/Owner/CEO (Retired in 2018)		**Rodney E. Thomas** Thomas and Herbert Consulting, LLC Management Consulting Co. Laurel, MD Co-Founder/Co-owner/CEO

* Deceased

Chapter 18

Our Educational Legacy: The Key to Unlocking Our Potential

Grandmother Fannie's diploma awarded June 13, 1900. This is the original sheepskin that was restored.

Sometime during the mid-1950s when she was clearing out boxes in a closet, where Mother stored a few photos and memorabilia, Jewel found Grandmother's original sheepskin diploma. Jewel was astounded to see this diploma, almost 60 years old, which was awarded to Grandmother Fannie Aribelle Williams by the Richmond Colored Normal School in 1900. Mother had been custodian of this treasured graduation certificate for some years, bringing it from Cary Street. Perhaps Mother had the document since living with her parents in the 1920s and '30s on Lakeview Avenue. However, the six of us never realized that this cherished artifact was in our midst.

Mother had told us that Grandmother Fannie had been a schoolteacher, but none of us, particularly the younger girls, really understood what a significant accomplishment this was for Grandmother Fannie to attend school in the late 1800s and complete her education in 1900. She had a high regard for educational achievement and set an excellent example for all of her descendants to emulate. Mother and Daddy had instilled in us a yearning for academic success and always encouraged our educational pursuits.

The Richmond Colored Normal School relocated several times and is now known as Armstrong High School. Annual reports from Grandmother's era include this statement about Armstrong: "The first class graduated at the close of the session 1872-73. Up to September 1908, there have been 821 graduates." It was remarkable that Grandmother was one of these graduates in that 35-year span that averaged 24 students each year.

She was hired in October of 1900 to teach in the West Point (Virginia) District, at School Number 9. One can assume that she was happy and excited to begin employment as a teacher. Grandmother Fannie was poised and refined and she was determined to teach basic skills. Unlike her mother, Mary Robinson Williams, Grandmother Fannie had never been enslaved, and now she and her sister Lillian Edith were among the small group of well-educated people in the city of Richmond, of either race.

Seemingly, Grandmother Fannie had faith and determination. We surmise that she did not know what conditions awaited her in West Point. Her contract stipulated that she would receive the "princely" sum of $20 each month, if money were available in the county treasury. Schools for Colored people were at the mercy of the White-controlled state government for funding and received far less financial investment than did White schools. These schools had fewer books, worse buildings and their teachers did not receive the same pay as White teachers. Out of her salary, Grandmother Fannie paid for room and board and any other ancillary personal expenses.

Her assigned school was likely ramshackle, as most facilities for Blacks were, and most of her students probably were poor. She was responsible for starting a fire in the pot-bellied stove each morning to warm the classroom, and cook the assigned menu of beans or some other filling food for her pupils' lunch. Her classroom was composed of children of varied ages and abilities, as was typical in such a rural area. Grandmother would do her very best to teach them all.

It is dubious that Grandmother Fannie ever imagined that she was to meet a handsome, smooth-talking, hardworking man there in this West Point community, who eventually loved her, married her and became our grandfather! After their marriage in 1902, her life as a "schoolmarm" would change forever. Grandmother Fannie, now married, no longer was permitted to teach in Virginia schools.

This pursuit of educational attainment has continued as Mother and her eldest sister, Aunt May, followed their mother's path. They were highly motivated to instill within their charges a love of learning and the development of critical-thinking skills. Aunt May taught in Richmond beginning in 1927, and later in Norfolk Public Schools until retiring in 1970. She was the epitome of an excellent teacher. She was always well prepared to teach academics, but went beyond those limits and took a deep interest in her students' personal development.

Despite teaching students who were impoverished, Aunt May identified their potential, believed in them, encouraged them and expected them to be successful. She was a strict disciplinarian who did not tolerate misbehavior in her classroom. At the same time, Aunt May was a concerned and loving teacher whom her students and their parents trusted, respected and loved. A number of her students and mentees made outstanding achievements. Among them were Dr. Yvonne Bond Miller, the first African American woman to serve in the Virginia State Legislature, first as delegate then as senator from Norfolk; and Dr. David T. Shannon, who became president of Virginia Union University.

Aunt May was well regarded by her fellow teachers and had an excellent rapport with the principals in the schools she served and especially with Miss Mary L. Coppage, principal at S. C. Armstrong Elementary in Norfolk, in the late 1940s–1950s, and later at Tidewater Park Elementary School. (S. C. Armstrong was formerly Cumberland Street School, Norfolk's first public school for African Americans built in 1886. Armstrong was razed to make room for a new city housing community and was replaced by Tidewater Park Elementary School during Norfolk's period of urban renewal.)

Our mother's kindergarten, which she operated in the early 1930s and reestablished in 1952, furthered the educational tradition. The gift of education that subsequent generations of our family inherited, motivated us to share and pass on our knowledge in a variety of environments.

Although Jewel did not select a teaching career, she recognized the importance of a college education. As a young girl, she observed that quite a number of women from the Black community worked as domestic help or in Richmond's tobacco industry. In the 1940s and 1950s, employment opportunities for Black women were very limited. On her trip to high school each day, Jewel saw very many women of our race waiting at a bus transfer stop heading to work in "White folks' kitchens" or in the local tobacco factory. She understood that this option was not for her, and stated early on, "Nobody had to convince me to go to college."

Jewel was prepared for a career as a teacher; nevertheless, she entered the federal government instead, and held personnel management positions where she was afforded numerous opportunities to instruct other employees.

Joyce, who graduated with a degree in physics, taught mathematics at Union-Kempsville High School in Virginia Beach for a year, beginning in 1963. She retired from the Maryland Higher Education Commission, having served for 27 years, and began employment as a substitute teacher in high schools in Anne Arundel County and worked there for six years.

Barbara, an English major, taught first at Armstrong High in Richmond. After moving to Maryland, she was a teacher in Annapolis, Baltimore and Havre de Grace Public Schools. Barbara then taught at Woodstock Job Corps and in other settings, preparing a diverse group of students for their GED examination. She collected Black history information and taught about it during Black History Month.

Betty, who majored in mathematics, had a long career in computer technology. Since her first retirement in 1998, she has worked as an adjunct mathematics instructor at Virginia Union, as a math substitute and tutor for Richmond Public Schools; and as a trainer with several major firms. On occasion, she currently tutors adults in computer technology and mathematics.

In their careers in nursing and as a watchmaker and jeweler, respectively, Lillian and Richard also were educators and trainers. Both taught new employees to acclimate them to their work and to improve skills necessary to perform their duties. In several positions Lillian held, she served as a nurse educator, advising her assigned patients as needed.

This education legacy continued in the fourth generation, as Barbara's daughter, Ta-Tanisha Nealy Walton, an English major, with an endorsement in early childhood education, started her teaching career at Norfolk's Tidewater Park Elementary in 1993. This is the school where Aunt May had taught more than 30 years earlier. Ta-Tanisha completed graduate studies and, since 1999, has held positions that have required increasingly significant management, academic and people skills. She continues her career with the Norfolk City Board of Education.

Aubrey Baden III, Joyce's son, began his teaching career as a teacher's assistant in 1993 while in graduate school. From 1999 through 2017, he taught high school English and literature at various schools in Rockville, Gambrills and Annapolis, Maryland. Currently, he teaches English and writing courses at Anne Arundel Community College.

Leonetty Gray, Betty's daughter, youngest in our fourth generation of educators, was a mass communications major, and since 2007, she has taught in the Richmond Public Schools, where she is positively impacting hundreds of young people. Leonetty serves as grade-level chairwoman for the seventh-grade team. She has coached basketball and served as liaison for the school's PTA.

Education is an enduring Waller value that all six of us siblings embraced. It was considered of utmost importance by every generation of our elders to encourage, and to even insist that we and our successors obtain an education. This tradition was begun by Grandmother Fannie in 1900, under enormously difficult circumstances, we are certain. Our parents' generation and each of us have been determined to sustain this precious educational legacy; to obtain all of the formal education we are able; to NEVER STOP LEARNING, to read, interact and gain new skills; and to use this knowledge and our FAITH to direct our lives. Certainly, 120 years later, in the Age of Information, education is even more essential.

Family Educators: Then and Now

Our only photo of
Grandmother Fannie
Williams Dungee,
about 1900

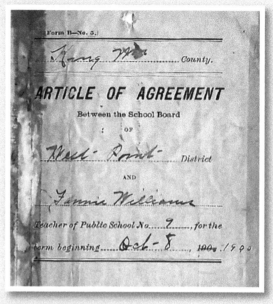

Grandmother's Article of Agreement to
teach in King William County, 1900 (Pg. 1)

An artifact we cherish:
Grandmother's school
bell from 1900

Agreement; note the monthly
salary of $20, "whenever there
are sufficient funds" (Pg. 2)

PRESENT PLAY — The Junior Primary Class of Randolph School presented Hansel-Gretel play in the weekly assembly at the school. The cast includes: Kerney Teele, Virginia Moore, Rachel Wilkins, John Dean, Alvin McGhee, Ollivene Womack, Yvonne Robinson, Zenobia Mitchell, Shirley Johnson, Katherine Spain, Eleanor Spain, Catherine Johnson, Julia Cousins, Jessie Warren, Charles Thornton, Lenord Forbes, James Fuller, Chester Ralph, Leroy Robinson, Daniel Jones and Nathaniel Scott. L. D. Henderson, teacher, directed the presentation. (Logan photo.)

Aunt May at Randolph School, Richmond, in the mid-1930s. Johnny Dean is in her class.

Mother and her kindergarten pupils on graduation day, mid-1950s

Lillian, Mother, Barbara, Betty; 2nd row: Jewel and Richard Jr., 1950s

MRS. ROBERT L. NEALY

Our sister, Barbara Waller Nealy, a teacher in Havre de Grace, Maryland

Barbara's daughter, Ta-Tanisha Nealy Walton, employed by Norfolk Public Schools

Joyce's son, Aubrey Baden III, a teacher in Anne Arundel County, Maryland

Betty's daughter, Leonetty Gray, a teacher in Richmond Public Schools

Our Parents Were Our First Teachers

Daddy's photo from
Armstrong Class of 1927

Mother's photo from
Armstrong Class of 1929

Armstrong High School
Class of 1927

Mother's Armstrong High
School Diploma, 1929

Armstrong
High School
Class of
1929

College
chums at
Virginia Union
University:
Mother and
Uncle John's
sister, Aunt
Mary, 1930s

Education Was the Key to Unlocking Our Potential

Richard Alexander Waller Jr.
Maggie L. Walker HS, '56
Richmond Professional Institute
Further Study for Jewelry and
Watch Repairing

Jewel Elizabeth Waller Davis
Maggie L. Walker, HS '56
BS, VUU '61
Further Study, George
Washington University

Joyce Dungee Waller Baden
B.T. Washington
HS, Norfolk, '59
BS, Norfolk State University
(NSU) '63
MA, University of MD
University College '87

*Lillian F. R. Waller Moore
B.T. Washington HS,
Norfolk, '62
AA, Prince George's
Community College '75

Betty Louise Waller Gray
Maggie L. Walker HS, '63
BS, NSU '67

*Barbara Florence Waller Nealy
Maggie L. Walker HS, '63
BA, NSU '67
MA, Coppin State U. '85

*Jean Marie Waller Brown
Armstrong HS, '55
BS, Hampton University '59
MA, Columbia University

Elsie Aretha Waller
Maggie L. Walker HS, '63
BS, Virginia State
University '67

Jean Frances Jones Waller
Brawley HS, Scotland Neck, NC '56
Smith-Madden Business School,
Richmond '59

LeCount Roscoe Davis Sr.
Armstrong HS,
Washington, DC '54
BA, MA, Southeastern U.
Washington, DC '60
Certified Financial
Planner Designee '78

Aubrey Garcia Baden Jr.
Wiley H. Bates HS,
Annapolis, MD '56
BS, Morgan State U. '60
Further study at
Howard University

**Richard Alexander
Waller III**
Jefferson Huguenot Wythe HS
Richmond, '81
BA, Virginia
Commonwealth U. '94

Robert Earl Thomas Jr.
Roosevelt HS,
Washington, DC '82
Attended NSU
Further Study at
University of DC

Rodney Erik Thomas
Coolidge HS,
Washington, DC '84
BA, University of DC '92
MBA, Howard U., '98

Aubrey Garcia Baden III
Queen Ann HS,
Upper Marlboro, MD '86
BA, Saint Mary's College of
MD '90
MA, U. of MD, CP '95

David Marcellus Waller
Richmond Community HS, '89
BA, Hampton University '93
Law Degree, Howard U. '97
Admitted: MD Bar '98,
DC Bar '00

Ta-Tanisha Nealy Walton
Woodlawn HS, Baltimore '89
BA, Norfolk State U. '93
MA, Norfolk State U. '99

**Ta-Tianna Nealy
McFadden**
Western School of Tech. and
Env. Science, Baltimore '97
BS, Norfolk State U. '03
MBA, Southeastern U.,
Washington, DC '08

Leonetty Akeisha Gray
Meadowbrook HS,
Richmond '99
BS, Norfolk State U. '03
MS, University of Phoenix '14

**Richard Alexander
Waller IV**
Albemarle HS,
Charlottesville '04
BA, Old Dominion U.
Norfolk '12

LeCount R. Davis Jr.
Winston Churchill HS,
Potomac '75
BA, MA, Middlebury College,
Middlebury, VT

*Garland Antone Davis
Winston Churchill HS,
Potomac '77
BA, West Texas A&M
University '81

Felandria Davis Coles
Winston Churchill HS,
Potomac '78
Attended Morgan
State University

Michelle Davis Martin
Winston Churchill HS,
Potomac '79
BS, College of William and
Mary, Williamsburg '83

Kim Lacy Waller
Thomas Jefferson HS,
Richmond, '81
BS, '85; MS, '94;
M.Ed., '00; Ph.D., '13;
Virginia State University

Evalena Foster Thomas
I.C. Norcom HS,
Portsmouth, VA '99
BS, Morgan State U. '03

*Carla Cousins Waller
Luneburg Central HS,
Victoria, VA '81
BS, VCU, '86
Further Study University
of VA, Charlottesville

Nataly Elizabeth Thomas
BS, University of DC '91
MA, U of MD University
College (UMUC) '98

**Olatungi "Valerie" Dove
Thomas**
BS Fourah Bay College
'94; University of Sierra
Leone, Freetown MBA
and MIS, UMUC '06

Tanya Miller Harris
MS, California State
University, Northridge, '00

Kweisi Thomas
Arundel HS,
Gambrills, MD '17

Hasani Thomas
Albert Einstein HS,
Kensington, MD '18

Sequoia Thomas
Arundel HS,
Gambrills, MD '19

*Ronald Erik Thomas
Largo HS, Largo, MD '96
Certificate,
Stafford Culinary
Arts School, '04

*Deceased

Joseph Francis Walton
BA, Hampton U. '92
AA, Gupton Jones Mortuary
School, '95
MA, NSU '05

Robert Lee Nealy
BA, Morgan State
University, '68
MA, Morgan State
University, '76

Epilogue

From January through October 2020, as we concluded the writing of our book, three major events occurred that have totally changed the structure of our entire society, perhaps permanently.

A Global Pandemic

The global COVID-19 pandemic was transmitted to the U.S. and was first discovered here in this country in January 2020. Starting in March, in response to the pandemic, all schools, business and social enterprises, churches, and other facilities, in the affected states began a full or partial shutdown in an effort to lessen the transmission of this disease. People were instructed to wear masks, to keep a social distance of six feet apart, to frequently wash their hands and to stay at home, except for essential purposes. COVID-19 was a new strain of the coronavirus for which there was no cure or proven treatment. Thousands became ill on both coasts and very many of these persons died, in spite of the heroic work of dedicated medical professionals and ancillary staff, which provided critical services in medical facilities. Despite the severity of the pandemic, there was no federal government policy to mitigate the disease or to provide for the procurement and distribution of medical equipment. Every state was on its own, and in competition for materials and supplies, such as ventilators and personal protective equipment (PPE).

There were those groups in society who could not be convinced that the pandemic was a reality, and they refused to follow guidance provided by the Centers for Disease Control and Prevention. Several governors did not mandate mask-wearing or social-distancing until well after the infection rate in their states began to rise exponentially.

Initially there was a proliferation of this virus among the elderly in nursing homes. In the U.S., COVID-19 was found to be particularly dangerous for Blacks and other people of color, who account for nearly 25% of those infected. Factors affecting this group are poverty, the presence of underlying health conditions, and inadequate health care resources available to them. There is an urgent need for the development of a vaccine and for therapeutics to treat this novel disease. Between February and September 2020, more than 7.1 million have tested positive for this disease and more than 200,000 have died in our nation. The U.S. accounts for at least 25% of the victims of this global epidemic, but has just 4% of the world's population.

Economic and Other Impacts of the Pandemic

Millions of people began to work from home and use technology. Millions more did not have that option, specifically persons whose jobs did not permit them to work from home, "front line workers." A majority of African Americans in the labor force were in this group. Small businesses, which supply 40% of U.S. jobs, were most adversely affected. As of this writing, many of these enterprises do not ever plan to reopen, despite grants and loans made available by the federal government. The temporary closure of nearly all businesses and a decline of up to 80% of travel, led to an unemployment rate of 14%, a level not seen since early in the Great Depression. The federal government, in late March, provided unemployment benefits to individuals and a stipend for each qualifying household.

Public and private schools were closed and education at all levels was made available online for all who could access it. The digital divide played a part in the limited access to online learning in poorer communities of all racial groups. For students who had previously depended on the school cafeteria for breakfast and lunch, some school districts found ways to still provide meals for pickup by the students' families.

Without employment, thousands of individuals were unable to purchase adequate sustenance for their families; food pantries, organizations and other entities throughout the nation attempted to fill some of this overwhelming need. For the first time, people who previously had been self-sufficient, now had to ask for food assistance. At some food pantries, the lines of autos stretched for several miles, as those waited to receive a box of food.

Further, family and social events of all types were canceled and most activities that occurred, such as weddings, funerals and meetings, were conducted using electronic media. The U.S. was forced into a "new normal."

Police Brutality and Protests

On Memorial Day 2020, in Minneapolis, Minnesota, George Perry Floyd Jr., a Black man, was killed by police during an arrest. This tragic event was captured on video by a bystander and was later broadcast around the world. The video showed that an officer held his knee on Mr. Floyd's neck for a period of eight minutes and 46 seconds, cutting off Mr. Floyd's airway, while three other officers held him down. During this time, Mr. Floyd begged for relief and said over and over, "I can't breathe." Observers demanded that the policemen release the deathly hold on Mr. Floyd, but to no avail. George Floyd had been arrested for allegedly using a counterfeit $20 bill to purchase cigarettes. He had not resisted arrest and had no weapons.

This murder by four Minneapolis policemen reignited the Black Lives Matter (BLM) Movement, which started in July 2013 on social media. BLM focuses on systemic racism and gun violence perpetrated by police and private citizens against African Americans. This protest followed the 2013 murder of Trayvon Martin, a Florida teenager, who purchased candy in a store near his home and was then approached and murdered by a self-appointed neighborhood watchman. More deaths of African Americans have occurred since. Many of the persons killed had no weapons, but were assumed to have committed a crime.

Now, however, the entire world witnessed George Floyd's tragic killing, and thousands were motivated to protest all across this nation and the world. Huge crowds of activists of all ethnicities marched together, carrying signs and demanding justice and the end of racism. Demonstrations occurred in urban centers and in small towns throughout the U.S. It is clear that institutional racism and discrimination have infected all of our culture for nearly 400 years. This had the impact of excluding Blacks and others of color from corporate boardrooms, as well as from almost every other center of power. Systemic racism has resulted in a lack of health resources, adequate food and housing, access to capital, quality education, employment opportunities that offer growth, and equal justice under the law. Urban renewal and new infrastructure for businesses and transportation have destroyed numbers of our neighborhoods and devastated the relationships within.

The massive protests that are now occurring are a force to be reckoned with by those in authority. These demonstrators have made demands that elicited rapid responses. For example, some cities are restructuring police departments. Others are removing Confederate statues, before the demonstrators tear them down. In a matter of a few weeks, government entities, businesses, and other organizations are beginning to modify and reassess their policies and practices. The majority of African Americans could not have envisioned this new awareness on the part of non-minority citizenry. It is heartening to witness.

Unlike the protests of the Civil Rights Movement of the 1960s, today many more people are re-examining their own attitudes. They are likely realizing the very negative influence of racism on the whole of society. We are optimistic and have hope for a more just nation. Our country is closer to the realization of its basic tenet as stated in the Declaration of Independence:

> We hold these Truths to be self-evident, that all Men are created equal, that they are endowed by their Creator with certain unalienable Rights, that among these are Life, Liberty, and the Pursuit of Happiness.

Effects of the Protests on
Waller & Company Jewelers

While the BLM and other demonstrators remained peaceful in their protest, unfortunately, some elements among the protesters resorted to violence and vandalism. Businesses were burned and looted and buildings were damaged. Even our small African American family business, Waller & Company in downtown Richmond, was affected when vandals broke the glass windows and door, smashed several showcases and stole watches and other fine jewelry. In the midst of this devastation, our brother, Richard, and other family members who are associated with the firm, were grateful for the assistance of local Divine Nine sorority and fraternity members. A number of them gathered at the store to offer their help and encouragement. *The Washington Post* on June 1, 2020, described the looting of Waller & Company during the protest and the subsequent help from loyal customers and friends in its article "Within the Wreckage of Richmond, One Small Miracle." Richard's photograph is also included in the article.

In recognition of Waller & Company's status as one of the oldest continuing small Black-owned businesses in Richmond, there has been substantial support from the city, local individuals, organizations, businesses and the media. Due to media coverage, local patrons and people from across the country were made aware of the company's setback. A number of them have contacted the store to express solidarity, to extend wishes for the business's recovery and to make purchases and donations to help restore it. The business is appreciative of the benevolence of these friends. Their responses affirm that kindness triumphs over adversity.

Local members of the "Divine Nine" historically Black Greek Letter sororities and fraternities who came to aid Waller & Company after it was vandalized and looted, May 31, 2020